The Greatest Secret in the World

To the greatest "success recorder"
in my life, with love . . .

                    . . . my wife, Bette

THE

GREATEST SECRET

IN THE WORLD

by

OG MANDINO

Featuring your own
SUCCESS RECORDER DIARY
With
The Ten Great Scrolls For Success
From
THE GREATEST SALESMAN IN THE WORLD

A World of Books That Fill a Need
FREDERICK FELL PUBLISHERS, INC.
NEW YORK

1,000,000 Copies in print

May 1972— 20,000 copies in print
January 1973—3 5 ,000 copies in print
June 1973—40,000 copies in print
October 1974— 80,000 copies in print
March 1975— 9 0,000 copies in print
October 1975—- 100,000 copies in print

For information address:
Frederick Fell Publishers, Inc.
386 Park Avenue South
New York, N. Y. 10016

Library of Congress Catalog Card No. 79-175423

Published simultaneously in Canada by
George J. McLeod, Limited, Toronto 2B; Ontario

Manufactured in the United States of America

STANDARD BOOK NUMBER 8119-0212-9

Words of Acclaim

The Greatest Secret In The World is inspiring. It's terrific! It motivates the reader to desirable action. Og Mandino, the author, is as unique and original as he was in *The Greatest Salesman In The World.*

He effectively extracts and combines many of the principles, techniques, skills and styles of authors who inspired and motivated countless millions to achieve physical, mental, moral and spiritual health . . . happiness . . . wealth and . . . success in their personal, family, social and business lives—authors such as: Benjamin Franklin, Norman Vincent Peale, Russell H. Conwell, Napoleon Hill, Frank Bettger, Dale Carnegie, Allan Fromme, James E. Allen and Lloyd C. Douglas.

> W. Clement Stone
> Chairman and Chief Exec. Officer
> Combined Insurance Company of America

☆ ☆ ☆

"This is an excellent book on successful living."

> Dr. Maxwell Maltz
> Author of Psycho-Cybernetics

☆ ☆ ☆

"The Greatest Secret in the World" gives you a program to lift yourself by your own bootstraps. If you have the guts to try it and to see it through, it will help you!"

> Edward R. Dewey
> President, Foundation For The Study of Cycles

This book will help you acquire the habits of success. It gives you a practical plan for internalizing the wisdom and ageless truth practiced by great men throughout history.

Just follow the simple instructions and you'll discover the greatest secret, which ought to be—but isn't—obvious to everyone. The *secret* unlocks a new world of exciting possibilities and extraordinary achievement that will amaze you.

Do more than read this book. Study it, use it daily and live the concept it teaches. Learn the greatest secret and put it to work for you.

Paul Meyer
President of Success Motivation
Institute Inc.

☆　　☆　　☆

"Og Mandino's track record testifies to the effectiveness of his philosophy. If he says he has a secret, you'd better believe it. If he offers to share it, listen."

Paul Harvey
Paul Harvey News
American Broadcasting Co.

☆　　☆　　☆

"I believe that those who will follow this book's program will move ahead. I have followed this kind of program without knowing it. Now, here it is for you. As a Christian I am a believer in God's love for us. I also believe we are expected to maximize our talents. The more successful you become, the more good you can do. Failures are not able to help others very much."

Richard M. DeVos
President, Amway Corporation

☆　　☆　　☆

"For four years, since first reading "The Greatest Salesman in the World" I have been hoping Og Mandino would produce a simple, concise manner in which salesmen, interested in their future and in their profession, could put into actual practice the principles and basic philosophy of the beautiful Scrolls. Now, with "The Greatest Secret in the World," he's done it! In a challenging and forthright manner he gives us a plan which, if followed, cannot help but change the entire pattern of a person's life—for the better —and transform him into a dynamic, new, wonderful force for good!"

Frank W. Errigo
Former Manager, U.S. Sales Training,
Parke Davis & Co.

☆   ☆   ☆

"Those of us who have been privileged to know Og Mandino over a period of years recognize in him a very wise minded and warm hearted man. An avid reader and lover of inspirational books, he gave us one of his own called "The Greatest Salesman in the World." The book became one of his best salesmen—a best seller. It provided us with ten scrolls for success.

"Now he gives us "The Greatest Secret in the World" which translates the principles of inspiration into practical guides for their application. Not just what to think and feel but more important, what to do and how to do it. In very simple terms and down to earth language, he provides us with a chart, a compass, a recorder and a reminder. He challenges and goads and encourages you every step of the way on your journey to the fulfillment of your best self on the road of life. An excellent companion for everyone who wishes to achieve success in all areas of human aspiration and activity."

Rabbi Louis Binstock
Temple Sholom, Chicago

"The Greatest Secret In The World" is an inspiring and affirmative guide to victorious living by the author that gave us "The Greatest Salesman In The World."

"Og Mandino emphasizes the basic steps which must be taken to make life worthwhile.

"This book is a guide to the happy practice of business faith as well as a manual for the use of that faith to solve the problems which surround us all."

Lester J. Bradshaw Jr.
General Agent, Continental Insurance Company

☆   ☆   ☆

"TREMENDOUS! THE GREATEST SECRET IN THE WORLD touches every area of life, it stirs and stimulates the mind, it tugs and warms the heart.

"Og Mandino has created another living classic that will touch the lives of millions through those who will be fortunate enough to be introduced to this book."

Charles "T." Jones
President, Life Management Services, Inc.

☆   ☆   ☆

"I'm happy to recommend THE GREATEST SECRET IN THE WORLD because it discloses not only the secrets of successful salesmanship but also of successful living. It's personal diary feature enables the reader to watch his progress toward success on a day-by-day basis and makes the book unique in its field."

Rev. John A. O'Brien, Ph. D.
The University of Notre Dame

"A fitting sequel to "The Greatest Salesman in the World," this book is a motivational step-by-step guide to success!

"This tremendously challenging book will inspire the reader to realize his moral, spiritual and financial goals.

"A 'must' for the library of everyone who sells—this includes us all."

Wallace E. Johnson, Vice Chairman
Holiday Inns, Inc.

Chairman of the Board
Wallace E. Johnson Enterprises, Inc.

☆   ☆   ☆

"Ever since I published Og Mandino's great work entitled The Greatest Salesman In The World, not a day has gone by without words of praise being heaped upon the book. The thousands of letters received could all be summed up with the recurring phrase, "It is the greatest course in self-improvement that one could take." At the time I brought the book out I predicted that it would become a classic. Now that I have been proved right, I can only say with all the sincerity at my command that Og's new book, The Greatest Secret In The World, will achieve the same status, and both books will live for generations to come."

Frederick V. Fell

The most valuable result of all education is to make you do the thing you have to do, when it ought to be done, whether you like it or not. It is the first lesson that ought to be learned. And however early a man's training begins, it is probably the last lesson that he learns thoroughly.

Thomas Huxley

The Legend Of The Ten Scrolls

From

THE GREATEST SALESMAN IN THE WORLD

Once up a time, nearly two thousand years ago, a young camel boy named Hafid fell in love with a wealthy merchant's daughter.

To improve his lowly station in life, in order that he could ask for the fair Lisha's hand in marriage, Hafid convinced his master, the great caravan merchant, Pathros, to give him an opportunity to prove his ability as a salesman.

From the caravan's supply wagon Pathros presented the youth with one new robe, which he challenged him to sell in the nearby village of Bethlehem. For three days in that poor hamlet Hafid failed in his every attempt to sell the robe . . . and finally, in a moment of pity, he gave the robe to warm a newborn baby in a cave near the village inn.

The young man returned to the caravan so full of shame and self-pity with his failure at becoming a salesman that he did not notice the bright star shining above his head which accompanied him on his return journey from Bethlehem.

But Pathros noticed . . . and the old man interpreted the brightness above as a sign from the gods . . . a sign he had been awaiting for many years . . . a sign which would release him from his secret possession of The Ten Great Scrolls For Success which he had received when he had also been a poor youth.

The old merchant, before his death, presented the ten scrolls to Hafid, who employed their principles to eventually become the wealthiest, the most successful, The Greatest Salesman In The World.

Several decades later Hafid passed the ten scrolls on to a very special person.

Now you hold them in *your* hands . . . and in this book you will be taught how to read them and how to apply their wisdom to your own life plus how to chart your day-to-day progress with your own Success Recorder so that you can achieve lasting wealth, health, happiness, and most important . . . peace of mind.

Chapter I

Before you and I become involved in the Ten Great Scrolls For Success, let's have a heart to heart talk.

I'll talk.

You listen!

The money spent on this book has been wasted.

Whether someone who cares for you, who wants you to "make it" big, who perhaps even loves you, gave you *The Greatest Secret In The World* . . . or whether you purchased it yourself . . . the money has been wasted.

The money has been wasted unless you are willing to accept, and try, a plan which has already worked for thousands of others.

The money has been wasted unless you have the guts, the persistence, and the will-power to follow the plan through to its fruition.

The money has been wasted unless you are willing to give the plan just ten minutes of your time *each day* of your work week . . . for forty-five weeks.

If I were a Nick the Greek-type-oddsmaker I'd say the odds were about 75 to 1 against your letting this system for doubling or tripling your income within a year help you as much as it can.

"But I'm different!" you remind me.

Really? If you made any New Year's resolutions last January 1st how long did you keep them? What about those excess pounds you were going to lose, or those cigarettes you were going to quit using . . . or that second drink you were going to stop having?

How long are you going to keep kidding yourself?

Perhaps you really do have a burning desire to succeed. Perhaps the added responsibility of marriage, or parenthood, or the desire for a new home, even a new car, or a mounting pile of debts have forced you to come to terms with yourself and acknowledge that the solution to all your needs and desires is really dependent on no one but you.

But a burning desire to succeed is not enough. As the Executive Editor of *Success Unlimited*, a magazine devoted to helping individuals improve their business and personal life, I long ago recognized the fact that there are two types of burning desire . . . and one type is phony and hypocritical. This phony type of burning desire is found in the person who is constantly telling his wife, his boss, and (worst of all) himself, that he really wants to succeed. He reads all the self-help books published and he gets his "kicks" from reading about others succeeding just as there are individuals who get their "kicks" from reading pornographic books. Unfortunately for our friends who read either types of these books they never get into action. They live their lives vicariously through their imagined participation in the lives and activities of others.

Tomorrow, to this type of dreamer, will be a great day.

Tomorrow never comes.

If I have struck a little nerve within you don't be concerned. Let me wipe that frown from your brow by assuring you that all of us possess some of that phony kind of burning desire. We make promises to others, promises that we know we can't keep, in order to get our boss or our wife off our backs . . . little realizing the harm we are doing to our own personality, because we *know* we're lying.

Today is the day you wipe that slate clean. No more phony promises, no more great plans in the evening which vanish when the sun rises, no more kidding yourself.

As you move, day by day, through this simple success program, you will slowly come to realize one important truth. *You are nature's greatest miracle.* Just to duplicate the computer you possess, called a brain, would require sufficient electronic equipment to fill the entire interior of the Empire State Building. You are rare and unique and the ultimate product of several million years of evolution. Both in mind, and body, you are far better equipped than Solomon or Caesar or Plato to make something beautiful and meaningful of your life.

You have a greater potential than anyone who has ever lived before you!

But you'll never "make it" by sitting on your duff and telling the world how great you're going to be, starting tomorrow. Sooner or later that friendly bill collector or landlord will shake his head at your promises. Sooner or later "credit" runs out. Sooner or later you "put up . . . or shut up."

This book will show you how to "put up" . . . if you will give it a chance to work for you.

The Greatest Salesman In The World, the book from which this guide was developed, has been a publishing phenomenon since its first edition in 1968. Few books, especially books on salesmanship, ever attain hard cover sales of a quarter of a million copies, and neither the author nor its publisher dared to imagine that a small volume about a salesman living in the time of Christ would be met with the enthusiastic reception that it has enjoyed. Even more amazing . . . sales have increased each year since its publication.

Executives responsible for the supervision of sales groups throughout the country quickly recognized the potential impact of *The Greatest Salesman In The World* as a motivational tool. Soon after its publication one firm purchased 30,000 copies! Copies have been purchased in volume by several hundred firms and sales organizations including such corporate giants as Coca Cola, Amway Corporation, Combined Insurance Company of America, Kraft Foods, Success Motivation Institute, Parke, Davis & Company, Sperry Hutchinson,

Volkswagen, Valley Steel Company, Genesco, Stanley Home Products, Norton International, The Southwestern Company, Stratford Squire International, American General Insurance Company of Delaware, Steamatic, Life Insurance of Kentucky, and Steak & Ale Restaurants of America, Inc.

Soon after publication, both the author and publisher received another pleasant surprise. *The Greatest Salesman In The World*, written primarily for sales people, had somehow filtered far beyond its intended market. Letters, seeking more information about the scrolls, began to arrive from individuals and organizations representing such widely diversified groups as: an artist colony, prison heads concerned with rehabilitation, management consultants, politicians, college professors, armed forces personnel, the medical profession, students, professional athletes . . . even a national center for brain-damaged children.

One salesman, after purchasing a gun to end his life because he had taken company funds, wrote that the book saved his life. He went to his firm, confessed his mistake, made restitution . . . and was given another chance.

Many wrote that the book's title was misleading. *The Greatest Salesman In The World* sounded like a "salesman's book" whereas it was a book for anyone searching for his or her niche in life. The book became, and still is, a popular gift item. Sales managers to their salesmen, parents to their children, wives to husbands who are still struggling.

Hopefully, with my "name-dropping" of all those cor-
porations and the other examples cited in the past few
paragraphs I have sold you on the fact that you are not
holding just another "how-to" sales book loaded with
complicated theories, charts, and selling techniques that
look and sound terrific but won't do much for you, tomorrow . . . or next week.

Each Success Scroll will be beneficial to you, no
matter what your profession may be . . . providing you
make one sincere promise to yourself . . . that you will
give it just *ten minutes* of your time, each work day, for
the next forty-five weeks. Ten minutes . . . about the time
it takes you to shower each day. Is that too much to ask
to double or triple your income in the next ten months?
When have you ever had a deal like this before?

Now, I'm not going to ask you what you want from life.
I'm not sure you could answer me. And I'm not going to
ask you to list your assets as they are now and then
make a second list showing what you'd like them to be
a year from now, five years from now . . . and so on. We
don't need to go through all that "pipe dream success
bookkeeping" you find in most self-help books.

All we both need to know are four facts. What is your
job title and what is your weekly income, today . . . plus
what would you like your job title to be and what do
you want to be earning forty-five weeks from now when
you complete your Success Recorder.

So . . . on a piece of paper, which I want you to keep
in the privacy of your home, I'd like you to write a memo
to yourself:

To: John Smith   Date:
My present job title is ....
My present weekly income is ....
My job title, 45 weeks from now ....
My weekly income, 45 weeks from now ....

That's all! Sign it . . . and tuck it away. Don't even
discuss it with anyone, except perhaps your wife. Do it
now . . . right now! Procrastination is one of your habits
we can't start working on any too soon.

Why didn't I ask you for a long list of the things you
wanted to achieve and acquire in the next 10 months?
Things like a new home, perhaps, or the beginning of
a college fund for your children, or maybe that movie
camera with a 10 to 1 zoom lens you've wanted for so
long? Because it wasn't necessary. If you have improved
your job title and your weekly income as much as I
think you've indicated on that private memo to yourself then all the material things you want will begin to
come your way. Any long list of your dreams is unnecessary! You know what you want . . . and your Success
Recorder Diary will help keep you on the right course.

Chapter II

Y ou can begin your Success Recorder on any Monday during the year . . . but once you commence you must not let anything except a serious illness prevent you from following through, each day.

One exception. If a vacation is on your schedule while you're working on this program go off and enjoy yourself. Then, on your first day back to work, just pick up where you left off.

You are about to read The First Great Scroll For Success. This scroll contains the instructions on how and when you are to read the scrolls that follow. Read this scroll several times during the week-end prior to the Monday you begin this program.

Warning! Don't let the simplicity of the scrolls' instructions turn you off. Simplicity is the keynote of success in any endeavor. Remember Vince Lombardi and his uncomplicated game plans relying on basic fundamentals and the minimum of plays. Remember the letters K.I.S.S. . . . "Keep it simple, stupid!"

You are about to learn how to tangle with the worst enemy you have . . . your bad habits. The Scroll Marked I contains the secret for getting rid of them. Read slowly.

Read with a pen or pencil in your hand, if you like, and underline ideas which you feel are most meaningful and relevant to you.

As you proceed you will discover that you have company. ME! I'll be with you all the way:

The Scroll Marked I

Today I begin a new life.

Today I shed my old skin which hath, too long, suffered the bruises of failure and the wounds of mediocrity.

Today I am born anew and my birthplace is a vineyard where there is fruit for all.

Today I will pluck grapes of wisdom from the tallest and fullest vines in the vineyard, for these were planted by the wisest of my profession who have come before me, generation upon generation.

Today I will savor the taste of grapes from these vines and verily I will swallow the seed of success buried in each and new life will sprout within me.

The career I have chosen is laden with opportunity yet it is fraught with heartbreak and despair and the bodies of those who have failed, were they piled one atop another, would cast its shadow down upon all the pyramids of the earth.

Yet I will not fail, as the others, for in my hands I now hold the charts which will guide me through perilous waters to shores which only yesterday seemed but a dream.

Failure no longer will be my payment for struggle. Just

as nature made no provision for my body to tolerate pain neither has it made any provision for my life to suffer failure. Failure, like pain, is alien to my life. In the past I accepted it as I accepted pain. Now I reject it and I am prepared for wisdom and principles which will guide me out of the shadows into the sunlight of wealth, position, and happiness far beyond my most extravagant dreams until even the golden apples in the Garden of Hesperides will seem no more than my just reward.

Time teaches all things to he who lives forever but I have not the luxury of eternity. Yet, within my allotted time I must practice the art of patience for nature acts never in haste. To create the olive, king of all trees, a hundred years is required. An onion plant is old in nine weeks. I have lived as an onion plant. It has not pleased me. Now I wouldst become the greatest of olive trees and, in truth, the greatest of salesmen.

And how will this be accomplished? For I have neither the knowledge nor the experience to achieve greatness and already I have stumbled in ignorance and fallen into pools of self-pity. The answer is simple. I will commence my journey unencumbered with either the weight of unnecessary knowledge or the handicap of meaningless experience. Nature already has supplied me with knowledge and instinct far greater than any beast in the forest and the value of experience is overrated, usually by old men who nod wisely and speak stupidly.

In truth experience teaches thoroughly yet her course of instruction devours men's years so the value of her lessons diminishes with the time necessary to acquire her special wisdom. The end finds it wasted on dead men. Furthermore, experience is comparable to fashion; an action that proved successful today will be unworkable and impractical tomorrow.

Only principles endure and these I now possess, for the laws that will lead me to greatness are contained in the words of these scrolls. What they will teach me is more to prevent failure than to gain success, for what is success other than a state of mind? Which two, among a thousand wise men, will define success in the same words; yet failure is always described but one way. *Failure is man's inability to reach his goals in life, whatever they may be.*

In truth, the only difference between those who have failed and those who have succeeded lies in the difference of their habits. Good habits are the key to all success. Bad habits are the unlocked door to failure. Thus, the first law I will obey, which precedeth all others is—*I will form good habits and become their slaves.*

As a child I was slave to my impulses; now I am slave to my habits, as are all grown men. I have surrendered my free will to the years of accumulated habits and the past deeds of my life have already marked out a path which threatens to imprison my future. My actions are ruled by appetite, passion, prejudice, greed, love, fear, environment, habit, and the worst of these tyrants is habit. Therefore, if I must be a slave to habit let me be a slave to good habits. My bad habits must be destroyed and new furrows prepared for good seed.

I will form good habits and become their slave.

And how will I accomplish this difficult feat? Through these scrolls, it will be done, for each scroll contains a principle which will drive a bad habit from my life and replace it with one which will bring me closer to success. For it is another of nature's laws that only a habit can subdue another habit. So, in order for these written words to perform their chosen task, I must discipline myself with the first of my new habits which is as follows:

I will read each scroll for thirty days in this prescribed manner, before I proceed to the next scroll.

First, I will read the words in silence when I arise. Then, I will read the words in silence after I have partaken of my midday meal. Last, I will read the words again just before I retire at day's end, and most important, on this occasion I will read the words aloud.

On the next day I will repeat this procedure, and I will continue in like manner for thirty days. Then, I will turn to the next scroll and repeat this procedure for another thirty days. I will continue in this manner until I have lived with each scroll for thirty days and my reading has become habit.

And what will be accomplished with this habit? Herein lies the hidden secret of man's accomplishments. As I repeat the words daily they will soon become a part of my active mind, but more important, they will also seep into my other mind, that mysterious source which never sleeps, which creates my dreams, and often makes me act in ways I do not comprehend.

As the words of these scrolls are consumed by my mysterious mind I will begin to awake, each morning, with a vitality I have never known before. My vigor will increase, my enthusiasm will rise, my desire to meet the world will overcome every fear I once knew at sunrise, and I will be happier than I ever believed it possible to be in this world of strife and sorrow.

Eventually I will find myself reacting to all situations which confront me as I was commanded in the scrolls to react, and soon these actions and reactions will become easy to perform, for any act with practice becomes easy.

Thus a new and good habit is born, for when an act becomes easy through constant repetition it becomes a pleasure to perform and if it is a pleasure to perform it is man's nature to perform it often. When I perform it often it becomes a habit and I become its slave and since it is a good habit this is my will.

Today I begin a new life.

And I make a solemn oath to myself that nothing will retard my new life's growth. I will lose not a day from these readings for that day cannot be retrieved nor can I substitute another for it. I must not, I will not, break this habit of daily reading from these scrolls and, in truth, the few moments spent each day on this new habit are but a small price to pay for the happiness and success that will be mine.

As I read and re-read the words in the scrolls to follow, never will I allow the brevity of each scroll nor the simplicity of its words to cause me to treat the scroll's message lightly. Thousands of grapes are pressed to fill one jar with wine, and the grapeskin and pulp are tossed to the birds. So it is with these grapes of wisdom from the ages. Much has been filtered and tossed to the wind. Only the pure truth lies distilled in the words to come. I will drink as instructed and spill not a drop. And the seed of success I will swallow.

Today my old skin has become as dust. I will walk tall among men and they will know me not, for today I am a new man, with a new life.

Now, before you continue, go back and read the scroll again. It contains one key sentence that I want you to underline:

"As I repeat the words daily they will soon become a

part of my active mind, but more important, they will also seep into my other mind, that mysterious source which never sleeps, which creates my dreams, and often makes me act in ways I do not comprehend."

In modern terminology what that key sentence means is that you are about to mind-condition yourself. You are about to begin the process of imprinting new relays and transistors onto your sub-conscious mind . . . that "control box" which mysteriously directs many of our actions and our ambitions. There's nothing weird or "far-out" about this technique. Many of the nation's outstanding examples of success constantly "program" themselves so that they instinctively react to various situations in a manner that will provide them with the greatest possible benefit. W. Clement Stone, Chairman of the Combined Insurance Company of America, and the country's outstanding expert on the motivation of others, used this technique on himself to amass a personal and self-made fortune of more than $400,000,000.

Perhaps your goal is not that high . . . but let's make a run for it, anyway.

Chapter III

Downhill ski racing is a battle of the individual against his environment . . . and the clock. What has always caused me to shake my head in sympathy for the losers is the infinitesmal difference in time between the winner and the also-rans.

The winner is clocked in 1:37:22 . . . one minute, thirty-seven and twenty-two one-hundreths seconds.

Second place is clocked in 1:37:25 . . . one minute, thirty-seven and twenty-five one-hundredths seconds.

In this case, the difference between being a champion and just another skier is *three one-hundreths of a second!* We can't even blink our eyes that fast.

What really was the difference between the champion and the also-ran? A lucky break? Maybe. But perhaps the champion practiced just a little bit harder . . . and just a little bit longer. Perhaps the champion worked on one bad habit, monotonous as this work is, until it was removed from his performance . . . saving him a fraction of a second on each downhill run . . . enough to spell success.

Now let's get to you . . . and let's start off by admitting that we both know you've got some, or many, bad

habits. Furthermore you know exactly what they are . . .
. . . perhaps procrastination, or over-indulgence, or lazi-
ness, or sloppiness, or a bad temper or an inability to follow through. I'm sure you can add to this list . . . and
I'm sure you also recognize that you're not going to get
very far so long as these vices are fouling up your
pistons.

I've always pictured George Washington as he looks
on my dollar bills . . . white coiffured wig framing a
face both calm, confident, and the personification of self-
control. My image of this great man was altered considerably when I read, recently, that George, in his
younger days, had a flaming crop of red hair . . . and a
temper to match.

Had George not learned to replace this bad habit with
one of self-control, which must have been extremely
difficult for him as he tried to lead an undisciplined and
untrained civilians' army against the forces of King
George, the odds are great that he would never have
become our first President.

Benjamin Franklin was probably the greatest and most
influential individual this country has ever produced.
He was "a man for any season," patriot, scientist, author,
diplomat, inventor, printer, and philosopher. He taught
himself to read French, Spanish, Italian, and Latin and
without his skillful guidance the United States might
never have attained its independence.

But even Benjamin Franklin had bad habits . . . and
he knew it. Unlike most of us, however, he determined

to do something about his. Inventor that he was, he worked out a "magic formula" to rid himself of his bad habits. First, he listed what he believed were the thirteen virtues necessary for true success: temperance, silence, order, resolution, frugality, industry, sincerity, justice, moderation, cleanliness, tranquility, chastity, and humility.

In his great autobiography he explained how he used the magic formula. "My intention being to acquire the habit of all these virtues, I judged it would be well not to distract my attention by attempting the whole at once, but to fix it *on one of them at a time;* and when I should be master of that, then to proceed to another; and so on, until I should have gone through the thirteen."

For another ingredient in his "magic formula" Franklin reached back to the advice of Pythagoras that it was necessary to examine one's actions each day. He designed the first Success Recorder:

"I made a little book in which I allotted a page for each of the virtues . . . and in its proper column, I might mark, by a little black spot, every fault I found upon examination to have been committed respecting that virtue upon that day."

Did the magic formula work for this great man?

Frank Bettger, author of one of the all-time classic books on self-motivation in the selling profession, *How I Raised Myself From Failure To Success In Selling* (Published by Prentice Hall) says, "When he was seventy-nine years old, Benjamin Franklin wrote more about this idea than anything else that ever happened to him in his entire life—fifteen pages—for to this one thing he felt he owed all his success and happiness."

Franklin wrote, "I hope, therefore, that some of my descendants may follow the example and reap the benefit."

Frank Bettger followed Franklin's examples, applied the magic formula to what had been a mediocre career as a salesman, and became the leading life insurance producer in the country.

Will the magic formula work for you?

Let's ask someone who can speak from experience and results. Let's ask the man we mentioned earlier, W. Clement Stone:

"Benjamin Franklin's magic formula has motivated many failures to subsequently succeed when they recognized, related, assimilated and used his formula. You can use it. Anyone can use it. I have never met a person who employed the principles in Benjamin Franklin's magic formula daily who failed to make progress toward the goals he was striving for. You have an absolute guarantee that any year can be your record year if you follow the principles of his formula daily."

In point of time it's a long journey from the ten scrolls which The Greatest Salesman In The World followed during the time of Christ, to Benjamin Franklin's formula, to the present day success of great achievers such as W. Clement Stone and Frank Bettger. And yet the principles have not been altered, even in the smallest way, by the passage of centuries.

THE GREATEST SECRET IN THE WORLD

The Magic Formula, or Success Recorder, or whatever name you want to give it, lives on . . . a proven and simple method which can change your life . . . if you give it the chance.

It always comes back to you, doesn't it?

Chapter IV

P ush-ups.

Let's think about them, for a moment, before we get involved in the next scroll.

If you got down on the floor, right now, how many push-ups could you do? Six, ten, twelve. Let's say you can do ten. Then, wait two weeks and try it again. How many? Probably ten, again.

But, if you do ten today, and try again, tomorrow, and the next day, and next, how many do you think you could be doing after two weeks? Probably thirty, forty, fifty, or more. Why? Because the muscles in your shoulders and your arms become stronger with each day's attempt. You are *conditioning* them to respond to a greater challenge each day and the daily increase in the number of push-ups you can do is only a small example of what you can accomplish in a specific period of time which, today, seems almost impossible. You are, indeed, a miracle of nature, and what applies to your shoulder muscles also applies to that big gray muscle between your two ears. And you are about to begin to make it do things which, at this moment, seem impossible to you.

Are you ready to begin?

Okay. Let's review the rules as they were spelled out for you in The Scroll Marked I. On the Monday which commences this program, sometime between your arising and departure for work you are to read The Scroll Marked II which you will find at the end of this chapter. Sometime around noon you are to read it again, which means you must take this book with you. Toss it in your brief case, perhaps, or leave it in your car if you use "wheels" in your business. In the evening, prior to your retiring, you are to read the scroll for the third time, and this time you should read it aloud. (You may have to explain this seemingly curious behavior to your spouse, but she's on your side and certainly wants you to make good.)

Following the scroll you will find your Success Recorder for the week, and the four weeks to follow, to help you live up to the injunction in The Scroll Marked I that each scroll is to be read, thought about, and acted on for thirty days.

Your Success Recorder was purposely designed to enable you to quickly conduct that "daily self-examination" which Benjamin Franklin insisted was an absolute necessity in a program such as this. In capsule form it summarizes the virtues, the qualities, the good habits, and the powers you are working to put into your life each day.

When your first day's work is done turn to your Success Recorder and place a date in the Monday section. Then, in the proper box, indicate how many times you read the scroll, that day. (Three, I hope.) Finally, read the review paragraph and consider how well you did in following the scroll's principles since you awoke. Rate yourself with 1 for "poor," 2 for "good," 3 for "very good," and 4 for "excellent." Be honest with yourself. Place your rating in the box . . . and tally the two boxes for the day. The highest rating you can have, for any day, is 7. This rating will serve as a daily and weekly accounting to yourself on your effort and your improvement.

Continue with this same procedure for the other four work days and then place the total number of points you earned for the week in its proper box. Then go on to the next week and continue this practice for five weeks . . . at which time you will begin a new chapter . . . and a new scroll.

Isn't that simple?

I'll let you in on a secret. It's so simple that it's going to "turn off" a lot of your reading companions of the moment who believe that nothing can be very worthwhile unless it's expensive or complicated. But then, they wouldn't be doing many push-ups either, if that was our program's purpose, so let them drop out with no regrets on our part. Mediocrity will always be their way of life.

As the first few weeks pass you will note a gradual change in both your attitude and your treatment of others, those you love and even casual acquaintances. You will begin hearing remarks like, "What's come over you?" or "That's not the old Smith I know!"

When that begins to happen you'll know the message of the scrolls and your daily Success Recorder review are beginning to work and your subconscious mind has been imprinted with new personality tracings that will disclose themselves time and time again in your future life . . . and you are on the way to a great year!

Now it's that first Monday.

As you begin this important day in your life I ask only that you remember these words:

"Failure will never overtake thee if thy determination to succeed is strong enough."

The Scroll Marked II

I will greet this day with love in my heart.

For this is the greatest secret of success in all ventures. Muscle can split a shield and even destroy life but only the unseen power of love can open the hearts of men and until I master this art I will remain no more than a peddler in the market place. I will make love my greatest weapon and none on whom I call can defend against its force.

My reasoning they may counter; my speech they may distrust; my apparel they may disapprove; my face they may reject; and even my bargains may cause them suspicion; yet my love will melt all hearts liken to the sun whose rays soften the coldest clay.

I will greet this day with love in my heart.

And how will I do this? Henceforth will I look on all things with love and I will be born again. I will love the sun for it warms my bones; yet I will love the rain for it cleanses my spirit. I will love the light for it shows me the way; yet I will love the darkness for it shows me the stars. I will welcome happiness for it enlarges my heart; yet I will endure sadness for it opens my soul. I will acknowledge rewards for they are my due; yet I will welcome obstacles for they are my challenge.

I will greet this day with love in my heart.

And how will I speak? I will laud mine enemies and they will become friends; I will encourage my friends and they will become brothers. Always will I dig for reasons to applaud; never will I scratch for excuses to gossip. When I am tempted to criticize I will bite on my tongue; when I am moved to praise I will shout from the roofs.

Is it not so that birds, the wind, the sea and all nature speaks with the music of praise for their creator? Cannot I speak with the same music to his children? Henceforth will I remember this secret and it will change my life.

I will greet this day with love in my heart.

And how will I act? I will love all manners of men for each has qualities to be admired even though they be hidden. With love I will tear down the wall of suspicion and hate which they have built around their hearts and in its place will I build bridges so that my love may enter their souls.

I will love the ambitious for they can inspire me; I will love the failures for they can teach me. I will love the kings for they are but human; I will love the meek for they are divine. I will love the rich for they are yet lonely; I will love the poor for they are so many. I will love the young for the faith they hold; I will love the old for the wisdom they share. I will love the beautiful for their eyes of sadness; I will love the ugly for their souls of peace.

I will greet this day with love in my heart.

But how will I react to the actions of others? With love. For just as love is my weapon to open the hearts of men, love is also my shield to repulse the arrows of hate and the spears of anger. Adversity and discouragement will beat against my new shield and become as the softest of rains. My shield will protect me in the market place and sustain me when I am alone. It will uplift me in moments of despair yet it will calm me in time of exultation. It will become stronger and more protective with use until one day I will cast it aside and walk unencumbered among all manners of men and, when I do, my name will be raised high on the pyramid of life.

I will greet this day with love in my heart.

And how will I confront each whom I meet? In only one way. In silence and to myself I will address him and say I Love You. Though spoken in silence these words will shine in my eyes, unwrinkle my brow, bring a smile to my lips, and echo in my voice; and his heart will be opened. And who is there who will say nay to my goods when his heart feels my love?

I will greet this day with love in my heart.

And most of all I will love myself. For when I do I will zealously inspect all things which enter my body, my mind, my soul, and my heart. Never will I overindulge the requests of my flesh, rather I will cherish my body with cleanliness and moderation. Never will I allow my mind to be attracted to evil and despair, rather I will uplift it with the knowledge and wisdom of the ages. Never will I allow my soul to become complacent and satisfied, rather I will feed it with meditation and prayer. Never will I allow my heart to become small and bitter, rather I will share it and it will grow and warm the earth.

I will greet this day with love in my heart,

Henceforth will I love all mankind. From this moment all

hate is let from my veins for I have not time to hate, only time to love. From this moment I take the first step required to become a man among men. With love I will increase my sales a hundredfold and become a great salesman. If I have no other qualities I can succeed with love alone. Without it I will fail though I possess all the knowledge and skills of the world.

I will greet this day with love, and I will succeed.

SUCCESS RECORDER
The First Week

❖❖❖

Monday   **Date**.............................   No. of times daily

1. I read The Scroll Marked II
        Review Paragraph for the Week
2. I greeted this day with love in my heart; I praised my
   enemies; I thought "I love you" silently to all I met and
   I loved myself enough to protect my body from overin-
   dulgence and my mind from evil and despair.

          (Insert number in each box)

Rating

Total

Tuesday   **Date**.............................   No. of times daily

1. I read The Scroll Marked II
2. I read the review paragraph above

Rating

Total

Wednesday   **Date**.............................   No. of times daily

1. I read The Scroll Marked II
2. I read the review paragraph above

Rating

Total

Thursday   **Date**.............................   No. of times daily

1. I read The Scroll Marked II
2. I read the review paragraph above

Rating

Total

Friday   **Date**.............................   No. of times daily

1. I read The Scroll Marked II
2. I read the review paragraph above

Rating

Total

Total points for the week

*Appointments for the week*_____

Monday_____
_____
_____
_____
_____

Tuesday_____
_____
_____
_____
_____

Wednesday_____
_____
_____
_____
_____

Thursday_____
_____
_____
_____
_____

Friday_____
_____
_____
_____
_____

*Achievements of the week*_____
_____
_____
_____
_____

Reflection For The Week

Love is never lost. If not reciprocated, it will flow
back and soften and purify the heart. —*Washington Irving*

SUCCESS RECORDER
The Second Week

❖❖

Monday   **Date** ....   No. of times daily

1. I read The Scroll Marked II
         Review Paragraph for the Week   **Rating**
2. I greeted this day with love in my heart; I praised my
   enemies; I thought "I love you" silently to all I met and
   I loved myself enough to protect my body from overin-   Total
   dulgence and my mind from evil and despair.
                    (Insert number in each box)

Tuesday   **Date** ....   No. of times daily

1. I read The Scroll Marked II
2. I read the review paragraph above   **Rating**

                                                    Total

Wednesday   **Date** ....   No. of times daily

1. I read The Scroll Marked II
2. I read the review paragraph above   **Rating**

                                                    Total

Thursday   **Date** ....   No. of times daily

1. I read The Scroll Marked II
2. I read the review paragraph above   **Rating**

                                                    Total

Friday   **Date** ....   No. of times daily

1. I read The Scroll Marked II
2. I read the review paragraph above   **Rating**

                                                    Total

                            Total points for the week

Appointments for the week_____

Monday_____

_____

_____

_____

_____

Tuesday_____

_____

_____

_____

_____

Wednesday_____

_____

_____

_____

_____

Thursday_____

_____

_____

_____

_____

Friday_____

_____

_____

_____

_____

Achievements of the week_____

_____

_____

_____

_____

_____

_____

Reflection For The Week

To each and every one of us, love gives the power of
working miracles if we will. —Lydia M. Child

SUCCESS RECORDER
The Third Week

❋❋❋

Monday   **Date**.............................   No. of times daily

1. I read The Scroll Marked II

> Review Paragraph for the Week

2. I greeted this day with love in my heart; I praised my   Rating
   enemies; I thought "I love you" silently to all I met and
   I loved myself enough to protect my body from overin-
   dulgence and my mind from evil and despair.   Total

(Insert number in each box)

Tuesday   **Date**.............................   No. of times daily

1. I read The Scroll Marked II
2. I read the review paragraph above   Rating

Total

Wednesday   **Date**.............................   No. of times daily

1. I read The Scroll Marked II
2. I read the review paragraph above   Rating

Total

Thursday   **Date**.............................   No. of times daily

1. I read The Scroll Marked II
2. I read the review paragraph above   Rating

Total

Friday   **Date**.............................   No. of times daily

1. I read The Scroll Marked II
2. I read the review paragraph above   Rating

Total

Total points for the week

Appointments for the week _____

Monday _____
_____
_____
_____
_____

Tuesday _____
_____
_____
_____
_____

Wednesday _____
_____
_____
_____
_____

Thursday _____
_____
_____
_____
_____

Friday _____
_____
_____
_____
_____

Achievements of the week _____
_____
_____
_____
_____
_____

Reflection For The Week

It is possible that a man can be so changed by love as
hardly to be recognized as the same person.   **—Terence**

SUCCESS RECORDER
The Fourth Week

❖❖❖

Monday   **Date**....................   No. of times daily

1. I read The Scroll Marked II
            Review Paragraph for the Week
2. I greeted this day with love in my heart; I praised my   Rating
   enemies; I thought "I love you" silently to all I met and
   I loved myself enough to protect my body from overin-
   dulgence and my mind from evil and despair.   Total
                        (Insert number in each box)

Tuesday   **Date**....................   No. of times daily

1. I read The Scroll Marked II
2. I read the review paragraph above   Rating

                                        Total

Wednesday   **Date**....................   No. of times daily

1. I read The Scroll Marked II
2. I read the review paragraph above   Rating

                                        Total

Thursday   **Date**....................   No. of times daily

1. I read The Scroll Marked II
2. I read the review paragraph above   Rating

                                        Total

Friday   **Date**....................   No. of times daily

1. I read The Scroll Marked II
2. I read the review paragraph above   Rating

                                        Total

                    Total points for the week

*Appointments for the week*_____

Monday_____

_____

_____

_____

_____

_____

Tuesday_____

_____

_____

_____

_____

_____

Wednesday_____

_____

_____

_____

_____

Thursday_____

_____

_____

_____

_____

Friday_____

_____

_____

_____

_____

*Achievements of the week*_____

_____

_____

_____

_____

_____

_____

Reflection For The Week

Love, and you shall be loved. All love is mathematically just, as much as the two sides of an algebraic equation. —*Emerson*

SUCCESS RECORDER
The Fifth Week

❖❖

Monday   **Date**...........................   No. of times daily

1. I read The Scroll Marked II
            Review Paragraph for the Week   ☐
2. I greeted this day with love in my heart; I praised my   Rating
   enemies; I thought "I love you" silently to all I met and   ☐
   I loved myself enough to protect my body from overin-
   dulgence and my mind from evil and despair.   Total
                              (Insert number in each box)   ☐

Tuesday   **Date**...........................   No. of times daily

1. I read The Scroll Marked II   ☐
2. I read the review paragraph above   Rating
                                                                ☐

                                                    Total ☐

Wednesday   **Date**...........................   No. of times daily

1. I read The Scroll Marked II   ☐
2. I read the review paragraph above   Rating
                                                                ☐

                                                    Total ☐

Thursday   **Date**...........................   No. of times daily

1. I read The Scroll Marked II   ☐
2. I read the review paragraph above   Rating
                                                                ☐

                                                    Total ☐

Friday   **Date**...........................   No. of times daily

1. I read The Scroll Marked II   ☐
2. I read the review paragraph above   Rating
                                                                ☐

                                                    Total ☐

                              Total points for the week   ☐

*Appointments for the week*_____

Monday_____
_____
_____
_____
_____
_____

Tuesday_____
_____
_____
_____
_____

Wednesday_____
_____
_____
_____
_____

Thursday_____
_____
_____
_____
_____

Friday_____
_____
_____
_____
_____

*Achievements of the week*_____
_____
_____
_____
_____
_____

Reflection For The Week

It is the duty of men to love even those who injure
them. —*Marcus Antonius*

Chapter V

S till with us?

Look around you. The group has thinned out considerably. Those that have already dropped out all came up with at least one excuse not to continue with their Success Recorder and it is not coincidental that this is the same group whose past performance shows the same "drop-out" habit in their previous attempts to make something of themselves. These are the individuals with the "phony" type of burning desire which I mentioned earlier. All talk . . . no action.

Of course, when you stop feeling sorry for them, the realization suddenly hits you that what they have done is make it easier for you. The competition is less. William Danforth, in his great self-help classic, "I Dare You," wrote that 95% of all individuals lack the determination to call on their unused capacities. This tremendous majority quickly settle on the plateau of mediocrity . . . and bewail their misfortune and "bad breaks" for the rest of their lives while the daring 5% continue on to leadership levels. He speaks to that small and surviving band of gutsy individuals, including you, when he says:

"The day of defending your present possessions is

gone. From now on you are not going to worry about holding your job. Put the worry on the fellow above you about holding his. From this day onward wrong things are put on the defense. You have marshalled right things for the attack. Your eyes are turned toward your strength, not your weakness. Henceforth, you will wake in the morning thinking of ways to do things, rather than reasons why they cannot be done!"

And henceforth, for the next five weeks, you will awake each morning to read and absorb the principles in:

The Scroll Marked III

I will persist until I succeed.

In the Orient young bulls are tested for the fight arena in a certain manner. Each is brought to the ring and allowed to attack a picador who pricks them with a lance. The bravery of each bull is then rated with care according to the number of times he demonstrates his willingness to charge in spite of the sting of the blade. Henceforth will I recognize that each day I am tested by life in like manner. If I persist, if I continue to charge forward, I will succeed.

I will persist until I succeed.

I was not delivered unto this world in defeat, nor does failure course in my veins. I am not a sheep waiting to be prodded by my shepherd. I am a lion and I refuse to talk, to walk, to sleep with the sheep. I will hear not those who weep and complain, for their disease is contagious. Let them join the sheep. The slaughterhouse of failure is not my destiny.

I will persist until I succeed.

The prizes of life are at the end of each journey, not near the beginning; and it is not given to me to know how many steps are necessary in order to reach my goal. Failure I may still encounter at the thousandth step, yet success hides behind the next bend in the road. Never will I know how close it lies unless I turn the corner.

Always will I take another step. If that is of no avail I will take another, and yet another. In truth, one step at a time is not too difficult.

I will persist until I succeed.

Henceforth, I will consider each day's effort as but one blow of my blade against a mighty oak. The first blow may cause not a tremor in the wood, nor the second, nor the third. Each blow, of itself, may be trifling, and seem of no consequence. Yet from childish swipes the oak will eventually tumble. So it will be with my efforts of today.

I will be liken to the rain drop which washes away the mountain; the ant who devours a tiger; the star which brightens the earth; the slave who builds a pyramid. I will build my castle one brick at a time for I know that small attempts, repeated, will complete any undertaking.

I will persist until I succeed.

I will never consider defeat and I will remove from my vocabulary such words and phrases as quit, cannot, unable, impossible, out of the question, improbable, failure, unworkable, hopeless, and retreat; for they are the words of fools. I will avoid despair but if this disease of the mind should infect me then I will work on in despair. I will toil and I will endure. I will ignore the obstacles at my feet and keep mine eyes on the goals above my head, for I know that where dry desert ends, green grass grows.

THE GREATEST SECRET IN THE WORLD

I will persist until I succeed.

I will remember the ancient law of averages and I will bend it to my good. I will persist with knowledge that each failure to sell will increase my chance for success at the next attempt. Each nay I hear will bring me closer to the sound of yea. Each frown I meet only prepares me for the smile to come. Each misfortune I encounter will carry in it the seed of tomorrow's good luck. I must have the night to appreciate the day. I must fail often to succeed only once.

I will persist until I succeed.

I will try, and try, and try again. Each obstacle I will consider as a mere detour to my goal and a challenge to my profession. I will persist and develop my skills as the mariner develops his, by learning to ride out the wrath of each storm.

I will persist until I succeed.

Henceforth, I will learn and apply another secret of those who excel in my work. When each day is ended, not regarding whether it has been a success or failure, I will attempt to achieve one more sale. When my thoughts beckon my tired body homeward I will resist the temptation to depart. I will try again. I will make one more attempt to close with victory, and if that fails I will make another. Never will I allow any day to end with a failure. Thus will I plant the seed of tomorrow's success and gain an insurmountable advantage over those who cease their labor at a prescribed time. When others cease their struggle, then mine will begin, and my harvest will be full.

I will persist until I succeed.

Nor will I allow yesterday's success to lull me into today's complacency, for this is the great foundation of failure. I will forget the happenings of the day that is gone, whether they were good or bad, and greet the new sun with confidence that this will be the best day of my life.

So long as there is breath in me, that long will I persist. For now I know one of the greatest principles of success; if I persist long enough I will win.

I will persist.

I will win.

SUCCESS RECORDER
The Sixth Week

❖❖❖

Monday   **Date** ....   No. of times daily

1. I read The Scroll Marked III
              Review Paragraph for the Week

2. I kept myself away from the sheep whose weeping and   Rating
   complaining are contagious; I avoided negative thoughts
   or words; I tried for just one more sale or completed one
   more task when it was time to journey home and I did
   not allow the day to end with a failure.   Total
                          (Insert number in each box)

Tuesday   **Date** ....   No. of times daily

1. I read The Scroll Marked III
2. I read the review paragraph above   Rating

                                                       Total

Wednesday   **Date** ....   No. of times daily

1. I read The Scroll Marked III
2. I read the review paragraph above   Rating

                                                       Total

Thursday   **Date** ....   No. of times daily

1. I read The Scroll Marked III
2. I read the review paragraph above   Rating

                                                       Total

Friday   **Date** ....   No. of times daily

1. I read The Scroll Marked III
2. I read the review paragraph above   Rating

                                                       Total

                          Total points for the week

*Appointments for the week*_____

Monday_____
_____
_____
_____
_____
_____

Tuesday_____
_____
_____
_____
_____
_____

Wednesday_____
_____
_____
_____
_____
_____

Thursday_____
_____
_____
_____
_____
_____

Friday_____
_____
_____
_____
_____

*Achievements of the week*_____
_____
_____
_____
_____
_____

Reflection For The Week

Every noble work is at first impossible. —*Carlyle*

SUCCESS RECORDER
The Seventh Week

❖❖❖

Monday   **Date**....................................   No. of times daily

1. I read The Scroll Marked III
                    Review Paragraph for the Week

2. I kept myself away from the sheep whose weeping and   Rating
    complaining are contagious; I avoided negative thoughts
    or words; I tried for just one more sale or completed one
    more task when it was time to journey home and I did   Total
    not allow the day to end with a failure.
                    (Insert number in each box)

Tuesday   **Date**....................................   No. of times daily

1. I read The Scroll Marked III
2. I read the review paragraph above   Rating

                                                        Total

---

Wednesday   **Date**....................................   No. of times daily

1. I read The Scroll Marked III
2. I read the review paragraph above   Rating

                                                        Total

---

Thursday   **Date**....................................   No. of times daily

1. I read The Scroll Marked III
2. I read the review paragraph above   Rating

                                                        Total

---

Friday   **Date**....................................   No. of times daily

1. I read The Scroll Marked III
2. I read the review paragraph above   Rating

                                                        Total

---

                            Total points for the week

*Appointments for the week*_____

Monday_____

_____
_____
_____
_____

Tuesday_____

_____
_____
_____
_____
_____

Wednesday_____

_____
_____
_____
_____

Thursday_____

_____
_____
_____
_____

Friday_____

_____
_____
_____
_____

*Achievements of the week*_____

_____
_____
_____
_____
_____

Reflection For The Week

The conditions of conquest are always easy. We have but to toil awhile, endure awhile, believe always, and never turn back.   *—Simms*

SUCCESS RECORDER
The Eighth Week

❖❖❖

Monday   **Date**............................   No. of times daily

1. I read The Scroll Marked III
           Review Paragraph for the Week

2. I kept myself away from the sheep whose weeping and   Rating
    complaining are contagious; I avoided negative thoughts
    or words; I tried for just one more sale or completed one
    more task when it was time to journey home and I did
    not allow the day to end with a failure.   Total
                    (Insert number in each box)

Tuesday   **Date**............................   No. of times daily

1. I read The Scroll Marked III
2. I read the review paragraph above   Rating

                                   Total

Wednesday   **Date**............................   No. of times daily

1. I read The Scroll Marked III
2. I read the review paragraph above   Rating

                                   Total

Thursday   **Date**............................   No. of times daily

1. I read The Scroll Marked III
2. I read the review paragraph above   Rating

                                   Total

Friday   **Date**............................   No. of times daily

1. I read The Scroll Marked III
2. I read the review paragraph above   Rating

                                   Total

                    Total points for the week

Appointments for the week _____

Monday _____

_____
_____
_____
_____

Tuesday _____

_____
_____
_____
_____

Wednesday _____

_____
_____
_____
_____

Thursday _____

_____
_____
_____
_____

Friday _____

_____
_____
_____
_____

Achievements of the week _____

_____
_____
_____
_____

Reflection For The Week

I hold a doctrine, to which I owe not much, indeed, but all the little I ever had, namely, that with ordinary talent and extraordinary perseverance, all things are attainable. —*T. F. Buxton*

SUCCESS RECORDER
The Ninth Week

✸✸✸✸✸✸✸✸✸✸✸✸✸✸✸✸✸✸✸✸✸✸✸✸✸✸✸✸✸✸✸✸✸✸✸✸✸✸✸

Monday   **Date**........................   No. of times daily

1. I read The Scroll Marked III
   Review Paragraph for the Week
2. I kept myself away from the sheep whose weeping and   Rating
   complaining are contagious; I avoided negative thoughts
   or words; I tried for just one more sale or completed one
   more task when it was time to journey home and I did
   not allow the day to end with a failure.   Total

   (Insert number in each box)

Tuesday   **Date**........................   No. of times daily

1. I read The Scroll Marked III
2. I read the review paragraph above   Rating

                                                 Total

Wednesday   **Date**........................   No. of times daily

1. I read The Scroll Marked III
2. I read the review paragraph above   Rating

                                                 Total

Thursday   **Date**........................   No. of times daily

1. I read The Scroll Marked III
2. I read the review paragraph above   Rating

                                                 Total

Friday   **Date**........................   No. of times daily

1. I read The Scroll Marked III
2. I read the review paragraph above   Rating

                                                 Total

                                      Total points for the week

*Appointments for the week*_____

Monday_____

_____
_____
_____
_____

Tuesday_____

_____
_____
_____
_____

Wednesday_____

_____
_____
_____
_____

Thursday_____

_____
_____
_____
_____

Friday_____

_____
_____
_____
_____

*Achievements of the week*_____

_____
_____
_____
_____
_____

Reflection For The Week

Persistent people begin their success where others
end in failure.   **—*Edward Eggleston***

SUCCESS RECORDER
The Tenth Week

✤✤

Monday   **Date** ....   No. of times daily

1. I read The Scroll Marked III
         Review Paragraph for the Week
2. I kept myself away from the sheep whose weeping and   **Rating**
   complaining are contagious; I avoided negative thoughts
   or words; I tried for just one more sale or completed one
   more task when it was time to journey home and I did
   not allow the day to end with a failure.   Total

(Insert number in each box)

Tuesday   **Date**....................   No. of times daily

1. I read The Scroll Marked III
2. I read the review paragraph above   **Rating**

                                   Total

Wednesday   **Date**....................   No. of times daily

1. I read The Scroll Marked III
2. I read the review paragraph above   **Rating**

                                   Total

Thursday   **Date**....................   No. of times daily

1. I read The Scroll Marked III
2. I read the review paragraph above   **Rating**

                                   Total

Friday   **Date**....................   No. of times daily

1. I read The Scroll Marked III
2. I read the review paragraph above   **Rating**

                                   Total

                        Total points for the week

*Appointments for the week*_____

Monday_____

_____

_____

_____

_____

Tuesday_____

_____

_____

_____

_____

Wednesday_____

_____

_____

_____

_____

Thursday_____

_____

_____

_____

_____

Friday_____

_____

_____

_____

_____

*Achievements of the week*_____

_____

_____

_____

_____

_____

Reflection For The Week

No road is too long for the man who advances deliberately and without undue haste; and no honors are too distant for the man who prepares himself for them with patience. **—Bruyere**

Chapter VI

Isn't this simple?

If you've come this far you already have the habit of reading your scroll three times a day. Nothing to it . . . just as there would be nothing to your doing a hundred push-ups by now if you had started that ten weeks ago. What a difference ten weeks makes!

And completing each day's Success Recorder . . . that's simple, too, isn't it? So simple that you can't even get out of doing it with the excuse that you're too busy . . . or too tired.

But do you realize what you have already done for yourself by simply reading and imprinting on your subconscious mind the words from The Scroll Marked II and The Scroll Marked III three times each day . . . for five weeks each? You are, no doubt, already communicating better with those around you, you have relieved friction from some quarters, and you have hardened that spine so that you continue to try, and try again when, in the past, you would have headed home afer a few failures, with your tail between your legs.

Now your personality is more open, you are a warmer person, you make friends easier, and yet you know how to hang in there until you make sales or complete tasks which you would never have come close to completing before you started this program. Furthermore, your sales or your duties are coming easier, because you're a friendlier and more likeable person, so you rarely have to call upon that new persistence you've developed. The scrolls, you are discovering, as with all virtues, are not separate, but related. When you improve on one they all improve. When one bad habit is subdued, the next is overcome with less struggle.

I told you that you were a miracle of nature . . . and now I'll prove it to you in:

The Scroll Marked IV

I am nature's greatest miracle.

Since the beginning of time never has there been another with my mind, my heart, my eyes, my ears, my hands, my hair, my mouth. None that came before, none that live today, and none that come tomorrow can walk and talk and move and think exactly like me. All men are my brothers yet I am different from each. I am a unique creature.

Although I am of the animal kingdom, animal rewards alone will not satisfy me. Within me burns a flame which has been passed from generations uncounted and its heat is a constant irritation to my spirit to become better than I am, and I will. I will fan this flame of dissatisfaction and proclaim my uniqueness to the world.

None can duplicate my brush strokes, none can make my chisel marks, none can duplicate my handwriting, none can produce my child, and, in truth, none has the ability to sell exactly as I. Henceforth, I will capitalize on this difference for it is an asset to be promoted to the fullest.

I am nature's greatest miracle.

Vain attempts to imitate others no longer will I make. Instead will I place my uniqueness on display in the market place. I will proclaim it, yea, I will sell it. I will begin now to accent my differences; hide my similarities. So too will I apply this principle to the goods I sell. Salesman and goods, different from all others, and proud of the difference.

I am a unique creature of nature.

I am rare, and there is value in all rarity; therefore, I am valuable. I am the end product of thousands of years of evolution; therefore, I am better equipped in both mind and body than all the emperors and wise men who preceded me.

But my skills, my mind, my heart, and my body will stagnate, rot, and die lest I put them to good use. I have unlimited potential. Only a small portion of my brain do I employ; only a paltry amount of my muscles do I flex. A hundredfold or more can I increase my accomplishments of yesterday and this I will do, beginning today.

Nevermore will I be satisfied with yesterday's accomplishments nor will I indulge, anymore, in self-praise for deeds which in reality are too small to even acknowledge. I can accomplish far more than I have, and I will, for why should the miracle which produced me end with my birth? Why can I not extend that miracle to my deeds of today?

I am nature's greatest miracle.

I am not on this earth by chance. I am here for a purpose and that purpose is to grow into a mountain, not to shrink to a grain of sand. Henceforth will I apply all my efforts to become the highest mountain of all and I will strain my potential until it cries for mercy.

I will increase my knowledge of mankind, myself, and the goods I sell, thus my sales will multiply. I will practice, and improve, and polish the words I utter to sell my goods, for this is the foundation on which I will build my career and never will I forget that many have attained great wealth and success with only one sales talk, delivered with excellence. Also will I seek constantly to improve my manners and graces, for they are the sugar to which all are attracted.

I am nature's greatest miracle.

I will concentrate my energy on the challenge of the moment and my actions will help me forget all else. The problems of my home will be left in my home. I will think naught of my family when I am in the market place for this will cloud my thoughts. So too will the problems of the market place be left in the market place and I will think naught of my profession when I am in my home for this will dampen my love.

There is no room in the market place for my family, nor is there room in my home for the market. Each I will divorce from the other and, thus will I remain wedded to both. Separate must they remain or my career will die. This is a paradox of the ages.

I am nature's greatest miracle.

I have been given eyes to see and a mind to think and now I know a great secret of life for I perceive, at last, that all my problems, discouragements, and heartaches are, in truth, great opportunities in disguise. I will no longer be fooled by the garments they wear for my eyes are open. I will look beyond the cloth and I will not be deceived.

I am nature's greatest miracle.

THE GREATEST SECRET IN THE WORLD

No beast, no plant, no wind, no rain, no rock, no lake had the same beginning as I, for I was conceived in love and brought forth with a purpose. In the past I have not considered this fact but it will henceforth shape and guide my life.

I am nature's greatest miracle.

And nature knows not defeat. Eventually, she emerges victorious and so will I, and with each victory the next struggle becomes less difficult.

I will win, and I will become a great salesman, for I am unique.

I am nature's greatest miracle.

SUCCESS RECORDER
The Eleventh Week

✦✦✦

Monday   **Date**...........................   No. of times daily

1. I read The Scroll Marked IV
           Review Paragraph for the Week
2. I refrained from all self-praise; I learned at least one new   Rating
    benefit or feature about the product I handle; I concen-
    trated on making each project or sales presentation better
    than the last; I worked on my manners and I kept the
    market place and home separate from each other in my
    thoughts.   Total

                          (Insert number in each box)

Tuesday   **Date**...........................   No. of times daily

1. I read The Scroll Marked IV
2. I read the review paragraph above   Rating

                                               Total

Wednesday   **Date**...........................   No. of times daily

1. I read The Scroll Marked IV
2. I read the review paragraph above   Rating

                                               Total

Thursday   **Date**...........................   No. of times daily

1. I read The Scroll Marked IV
2. I read the review paragraph above   Rating

                                               Total

Friday   **Date**...........................   No. of times daily

1. I read The Scroll Marked IV
2. I read the review paragraph above   Rating

                                               Total

                          Total points for the week

Appointments for the week _____

Monday _____

_____
_____
_____
_____

Tuesday _____

_____
_____
_____
_____

Wednesday _____

_____
_____
_____
_____

Thursday _____

_____
_____
_____
_____

Friday _____

_____
_____
_____
_____

Achievements of the week _____

_____
_____
_____
_____
_____
_____

Reflection For The Week

Man is an animal which alone among the animals re-
fuses to be satisfied by the fulfillment of animal desires.
—*Alexander Graham Bell*

SUCCESS RECORDER
The Twelfth Week

❖❖

Monday　　　　　　　　　**Date**...........................　　No. of times daily

1. I read The Scroll Marked IV
　　　　　Review Paragraph for the Week
2. I refrained from all self-praise; I learned at least one new　　**Rating**
benefit or feature about the product I handle; I concentrated on making each project or sales presentation better
than the last; I worked on my manners and I kept the
market place and home separate from each other in my
thoughts.　　　　　　　　　　　　　　　　　　　Total

(Insert number in each box)

Tuesday　　　　　　　　　**Date**...........................　　No. of times daily

1. I read The Scroll Marked IV
2. I read the review paragraph above　　**Rating**

　　　　　　　　　　　　　　　　Total

Wednesday　　　　　　　　**Date**...........................　　No. of times daily

1. I read The Scroll Marked IV
2. I read the review paragraph above　　**Rating**

　　　　　　　　　　　　　　　　Total

Thursday　　　　　　　　　**Date**...........................　　No. of times daily

1. I read The Scroll Marked IV
2. I read the review paragraph above　　**Rating**

　　　　　　　　　　　　　　　　Total

Friday　　　　　　　　　　**Date**...........................　　No. of times daily

1. I read The Scroll Marked IV
2. I read the review paragraph above　　**Rating**

　　　　　　　　　　　　　　　　Total

　　　　　　　　　　Total points for the week

Appointments for the week_____

Monday_____

_____
_____
_____
_____

Tuesday_____

_____
_____
_____
_____

Wednesday_____

_____
_____
_____
_____

Thursday_____

_____
_____
_____
_____

Friday_____

_____
_____
_____
_____

Achievements of the week_____

_____
_____
_____
_____

Reflection For The Week

Whoever considers the study of anatomy, I believe, will never be an atheist; the frame of man's body, and coherence of his parts, being so strange and paradoxical, that I hold it to be the greatest miracle of nature.　　　　**—Lord Herbert**

SUCCESS RECORDER

The Thirteenth Week

✤✤

Monday **Date**.................................. No. of times daily

1. I read The Scroll Marked IV ☐

Review Paragraph for the Week

2. I refrained from all self-praise; I learned at least one new benefit or feature about the product I handle; I concentrated on making each project or sales presentation better than the last; I worked on my manners and I kept the market place and home separate from each other in my thoughts. Rating ☐

Total

(Insert number in each box) ☐

Tuesday **Date**.................................. No. of times daily

1. I read The Scroll Marked IV ☐
2. I read the review paragraph above

Rating ☐

Total ☐

Wednesday **Date**.................................. No. of times daily

1. I read The Scroll Marked IV ☐
2. I read the review paragraph above

Rating ☐

Total ☐

Thursday **Date**.................................. No. of times daily

1. I read The Scroll Marked IV ☐
2. I read the review paragraph above

Rating ☐

Total ☐

Friday **Date**.................................. No. of times daily

1. I read The Scroll Marked IV ☐
2. I read the review paragraph above

Rating ☐

Total ☐

Total points for the week ☐

*Appointments for the week*_____

Monday_____
_____
_____
_____
_____
_____

Tuesday_____
_____
_____
_____
_____

Wednesday_____
_____
_____
_____
_____

Thursday_____
_____
_____
_____
_____

Friday_____
_____
_____
_____

*Achievements of the week*_____
_____
_____
_____
_____
_____
_____

Reflection For The Week

The way of a superior man is threefold: virtuous, he is free from anxieties; wise, he is free from perplexities; bold, he is free from fear.
—**Confucius**

SUCCESS RECORDER
The Fourteenth Week

❖❖

Monday   **Date**...............................   No. of times daily

1. I read The Scroll Marked IV
          Review Paragraph for the Week
2. I refrained from all self-praise; I learned at least one new   Rating
   benefit or feature about the product I handle; I concentrated on making each project or sales presentation better
   than the last; I worked on my manners and I kept the
   market place and home separate from each other in my
   thoughts.   Total

(Insert number in each box)

Tuesday   **Date**...............................   No. of times daily

1. I read The Scroll Marked IV
2. I read the review paragraph above   Rating

Total

Wednesday   **Date**...............................   No. of times daily

1. I read The Scroll Marked IV
2. I read the review paragraph above   Rating

Total

Thursday   **Date**...............................   No. of times daily

1. I read The Scroll Marked IV
2. I read the review paragraph above   Rating

Total

Friday   **Date**...............................   No. of times daily

1. I read The Scroll Marked IV
2. I read the review paragraph above   Rating

Total

Total points for the week

*Appointments for the week*_____

Monday_____
_____
_____
_____
_____

Tuesday_____
_____
_____
_____
_____

Wednesday_____
_____
_____
_____
_____

Thursday_____
_____
_____
_____
_____

Friday_____
_____
_____
_____
_____

*Achievements of the week*_____
_____
_____
_____
_____
_____

Reflection For The Week

I mean to make myself a man, and if I succeed in
that, I shall succeed in everything else.   —*Garfield*

SUCCESS RECORDER
The Fifteenth Week

❖❖

Monday   **Date**............................   No. of times daily

1. I read The Scroll Marked IV
           Review Paragraph for the Week
2. I refrained from all self-praise; I learned at least one new   Rating
   benefit or feature about the product I handle; I concentrated on making each project or sales presentation better
   than the last; I worked on my manners and I kept the
   market place and home separate from each other in my
   thoughts.   Total

(Insert number in each box)

Tuesday   **Date**............................   No. of times daily

1. I read The Scroll Marked IV
2. I read the review paragraph above   Rating

   Total

Wednesday   **Date**............................   No. of times daily

1. I read The Scroll Marked IV
2. I read the review paragraph above   Rating

   Total

Thursday   **Date**............................   No. of times daily

1. I read The Scroll Marked IV
2. I read the review paragraph above   Rating

   Total

Friday   **Date**............................   No. of times daily

1. I read The Scroll Marked IV
2. I read the review paragraph above   Rating

   Total

Total points for the week

*Appointments for the week*_____

Monday_____
_____
_____
_____
_____

Tuesday_____
_____
_____
_____
_____

Wednesday_____
_____
_____
_____

Thursday_____
_____
_____
_____
_____

Friday_____
_____
_____
_____
_____

*Achievements of the week*_____
_____
_____
_____
_____
_____

Reflection For The Week

Man himself is the crowning wonder of creation; the
study of his nature the noblest study the world affords.
—Gladstone

Chapter VII

Fifteen weeks have now passed.

You have come a long way, my good friend.

If you have read the scrolls three times a day; if you have taken a few moments each evening to examine your actions of the day . . . then without doubt you are a changed person from the individual you were. And isn't it amazing . . . everyone around you seems to have changed, too.

Perhaps this old legend will help you understand what has happened to you:

There was an old Quaker who stood at the village well, greeting weary travelers who passed along the way. And to each who asked, "What manner of people live hereabouts?" he would respond with another question, "What manner of people did thee find in thy last abode?"

If the traveler said that he had left a community where people were bright and gay; genial and fun-loving, the Quaker would answer confidently that the questing one would find them much the same in his community. But to travelers who complained that they left a community where people were ugly, quarrelsome, and ill-tempered, the patriarch would sadly shake his head and say "Alas, here thee will find them much the same."

You are about to embark on five very interesting weeks. More than any other scroll, I promise you that as you begin to live the injunctions in The Scroll Marked V you will be noticed by strangers, friends, and foes alike.

Henry Van Dyke once wrote that some people are so afraid to die that they never begin to live. For the next five weeks you are being asked to imagine that each day, when you arise, will be your last day on earth . . . and you are to act accordingly.

Those with little faith, and less courage, would shrivel up in a corner if they knew this was really their last day on earth . . . but since you have persisted to this point with your Success Recorder I have little doubt of your abundance of faith . . . or courage.

You may wish to keep additional notes about how others react to you during these next five weeks . . . especially those above you in the "pecking order" of your company. Along with what you have *already* accomplished in transforming your personality, these weeks usually produce confrontations with superiors which lead to interesting developments . . . like promotions and raises.

So let's get started with this important scroll:

The Scroll Marked V

I will live this day as if it is my last.

And what shall I do with this last precious day which remains in my keeping? First, I will seal up its container of life so that not one drop spills itself upon the sand. I will waste not a moment mourning yesterday's misfortunes, yesterday's defeats, yesterday's aches of the heart, for why should I throw good after bad?

Can sand flow upward in the hour glass? Will the sun rise where it sets and set where it rises? Can I relive the errors of yesterday and right them? Can I call back yesterday's wounds and make them whole? Can I become younger than yesterday? Can I take back the evil that was spoken, the blows that were struck, the pain that was caused? No. Yesterday is buried forever and I will think of it no more.

I will live this day as if it is my last.

And what then shall I do? Forgetting yesterday neither will I think of tomorrow. Why should I throw *now* after *maybe?* Can tomorrow's sand flow through the glass before today's? Will the sun rise twice this morning? Can I perform tomorrow's deeds while standing in today's path? Can I place tomorrow's gold in today's purse? Can tomorrow's child be born today? Can tomorrow's death cast its shadow backward and darken today's joy? Should I concern myself over events which I may never witness? Should I torment myself with problems that may never come to pass? No! Tomorrow lies buried with yesterday, and I will think of it no more.

I will live this day as if it is my last.

This day is all I have and these hours are now my eternity. I greet this sunrise with cries of joy as a prisoner who is reprieved from death. I lift mine arms with thanks for this priceless gift of a new day. So too, I will beat upon my heart with gratitude as I consider all who greeted yesterday's sunrise who are no longer with the living today. I am indeed a fortunate man and today's hours are but a bonus, undeserved. Why have I been allowed to live this extra day when others, far better than I, have departed? Is it that they have accomplished their purpose while mine is yet to be achieved? Is this another opportunity for me to become the man I know I can be? Is there a purpose in nature? Is this my day to excel?

I will live this day as if it is my last.

I have but one life and life is naught but a measurement of time. When I waste one I destroy the other. If I waste today I destroy the last page of my life. Therefore, each hour of this day will I cherish for it can never return. It cannot be banked today to be withdrawn on the morrow, for who can trap the wind? Each minute of this day will I grasp with both hands and fondle with love for its value is beyond price. What dying man can purchase another breath though he willingly give all his gold? What price dare I place on the hours ahead? I will make them priceless!

I will live this day as if it is my last.

I will avoid with fury the killers of time. Procrastination I will destroy with action; doubt I will bury under faith; fear I will dismember with confidence. Where there are idle mouths I will listen not; where there are idle hands I will linger not; where there are idle bodies I will visit not. Henceforth I know that to court idleness is to steal food, clothing, and warmth from those I love. I am not a thief. I am a man of love and today is my last chance to prove my love and my greatness.

I will live this day as if it is my last.

The duties of today I shall fulfill today. Today I shall fondle my children while they are young; tomorrow they will be gone, and so will I. Today I shall embrace my woman with sweet kisses; tomorrow she will be gone, and so will I. Today I shall lift up a friend in need; tomorrow he will no longer cry for help, nor will I hear his cries. Today I shall give myself in sacrifice and work; tomorrow I will have nothing to give, and there will be none to receive.

I will live this day as if it is my last.

And if it is my last, it will be my greatest monument. This day I will make the best day of my life. This day I will drink every minute to its full. I will savor its taste and give thanks. I will maketh every hour count and each minute I will trade only for something of value. I will labor harder than ever before and push my muscles until they cry for relief, and then I will continue. I will make more calls than ever before. I will sell more goods than ever before. I will earn more gold than ever before. Each minute of today will be more fruitful than hours of yesterday. My last must be my best.

I will live this day as if it is my last.

And if it is not, I shall fall to my knees and give thanks.

SUCCESS RECORDER
The Sixteenth Week

❋❋

Monday   **Date**................................   No. of times daily

1. I read The Scroll Marked V
       Review Paragraph for the Week
2. I greeted this morning with gratitude for the gift of another day; I mourned not yesterday's mistakes and defeats; I wasted none of my precious time on foolishness;
I treated everyone with tenderness as if I would see them
no more and I truly lived this day as if it were my last.

Rating

Total

(Insert number in each box)

Tuesday   **Date**................................   No. of times daily

1. I read The Scroll Marked V
2. I read the review paragraph above

Rating

Total

Wednesday   **Date**................................   No. of times daily

1. I read The Scroll Marked V
2. I read the review paragraph above

Rating

Total

Thursday   **Date**................................   No. of times daily

1. I read The Scroll Marked V
2. I read the review paragraph above

Rating

Total

Friday   **Date**................................   No. of times daily

1. I read The Scroll Marked V
2. I read the review paragraph above

Rating

Total

Total points for the week

Appointments for the week_____

Monday_____
_____
_____
_____
_____

Tuesday_____
_____
_____
_____
_____

Wednesday_____
_____
_____
_____
_____

Thursday_____
_____
_____
_____
_____

Friday_____
_____
_____
_____
_____

Achievements of the week_____
_____
_____
_____
_____
_____

Reflection For The Week

The life of every man is a diary in which he means to write one story, and writes another; and his humblest hour is when he compares the volume as it is with what he hoped to make it. —*James M. Barrie*

SUCCESS RECORDER
The Seventeenth Week

❖❖

Monday   **Date**.............................   No. of times daily

1. I read The Scroll Marked V
   Review Paragraph for the Week
2. I greeted this morning with gratitude for the gift of another day; I mourned not yesterday's mistakes and defeats; I wasted none of my precious time on foolishness;
   I treated everyone with tenderness as if I would see them
   no more and I truly lived this day as if it were my last.
   (Insert number in each box)

Rating

Total

Tuesday   **Date**.............................   No. of times daily

1. I read The Scroll Marked V
2. I read the review paragraph above

Rating

Total

Wednesday   **Date**.............................   No. of times daily

1. I read The Scroll Marked V
2. I read the review paragraph above

Rating

Total

Thursday   **Date**.............................   No. of times daily

1. I read The Scroll Marked V
2. I read the review paragraph above

Rating

Total

Friday   **Date**.............................   No. of times daily

1. I read The Scroll Marked V
2. I read the review paragraph above

Rating

Total

Total points for the week

*Appointments for the week*_____

Monday_____
_____
_____
_____
_____

Tuesday_____
_____
_____
_____
_____

Wednesday_____
_____
_____
_____
_____

Thursday_____
_____
_____
_____
_____

Friday_____
_____
_____
_____
_____

*Achievements of the week*_____
_____
_____
_____
_____

Reflection For The Week

There is no cure for birth and death save to enjoy the interval. The dark background which death supplies brings out the tender colors of life in all their purity.

—*George Santayana*

SUCCESS RECORDER
The Eighteenth Week

✤✤

Monday   **Date**................................   No. of times daily

1. I read The Scroll Marked V
        Review Paragraph for the Week
2. I greeted this morning with gratitude for the gift of an-   Rating
    other day; I mourned not yesterday's mistakes and de-
    feats; I wasted none of my precious time on foolishness;
    I treated everyone with tenderness as if I would see them
    no more and I truly lived this day as if it were my last.   Total
                    (Insert number in each box)

Tuesday   **Date**................................   No. of times daily

1. I read The Scroll Marked V
2. I read the review paragraph above   Rating

                                        Total

Wednesday   **Date**................................   No. of times daily

1. I read The Scroll Marked V
2. I read the review paragraph above   Rating

                                        Total

Thursday   **Date**................................   No. of times daily

1. I read The Scroll Marked V
2. I read the review paragraph above   Rating

                                        Total

Friday   **Date**................................   No. of times daily

1. I read The Scroll Marked V
2. I read the review paragraph above   Rating

                                        Total

                    Total points for the week

*Appointments for the week*_____

Monday_____
_____
_____
_____
_____
_____

Tuesday_____
_____
_____
_____
_____
_____

Wednesday_____
_____
_____
_____
_____
_____

Thursday_____
_____
_____
_____
_____
_____

Friday_____
_____
_____
_____
_____
_____

*Achievements of the week*_____
_____
_____
_____

Reflection For The Week

When I reflect, as I frequently do, upon the felicity I have enjoyed, I sometimes say to myself, that were the offer made me, I would engage to run again, from beginning to end, the same career of life. All I would ask, should be the privilege of an author, to correct in a second edition, certain errors of the first.

—*Benjamin Franklin*

SUCCESS RECORDER
The Nineteenth Week

❋❋

Monday **Date**................................ No. of times daily

1. I read The Scroll Marked V
   Review Paragraph for the Week
2. I greeted this morning with gratitude for the gift of another day; I mourned not yesterday's mistakes and defeats; I wasted none of my precious time on foolishness;
   I treated everyone with tenderness as if I would see them
   no more and I truly lived this day as if it were my last.
   (Insert number in each box)

Rating

Total

Tuesday **Date**................................ No. of times daily

1. I read The Scroll Marked V
2. I read the review paragraph above

Rating

Total

Wednesday **Date**................................ No. of times daily

1. I read The Scroll Marked V
2. I read the review paragraph above

Rating

Total

Thursday **Date**................................ No. of times daily

1. I read The Scroll Marked V
2. I read the review paragraph above

Rating

Total

Friday **Date**................................ No. of times daily

1. I read The Scroll Marked V
2. I read the review paragraph above

Rating

Total

Total points for the week

Appointments for the week _____

Monday _____
_____
_____
_____
_____

Tuesday _____
_____
_____
_____
_____

Wednesday _____
_____
_____
_____
_____

Thursday _____
_____
_____
_____
_____

Friday _____
_____
_____
_____
_____

Achievements of the week _____

_____
_____
_____
_____
_____

Reflection For The Week

I count all that part of my life lost which I spent not
in communion with God, or in doing good.   —Donne

SUCCESS RECORDER
The Twentieth Week

✥✥

Monday　　　　　　**Date**.................................　No. of times daily

1. I read The Scroll Marked V
   　　　　Review Paragraph for the Week
2. I greeted this morning with gratitude for the gift of an-　Rating
   other day; I mourned not yesterday's mistakes and defeats; I wasted none of my precious time on foolishness;
   I treated everyone with tenderness as if I would see them
   no more and I truly lived this day as if it were my last.　Total
   　　　　　　　(Insert number in each box)

Tuesday　　　　　　**Date**.................................　No. of times daily

1. I read The Scroll Marked V
2. I read the review paragraph above　Rating

　　　　　　　　　　　　　　　　Total

Wednesday　　　　　**Date**.................................　No. of times daily

1. I read The Scroll Marked V
2. I read the review paragraph above　Rating

　　　　　　　　　　　　　　　　Total

Thursday　　　　　　**Date**.................................　No. of times daily

1. I read The Scroll Marked V
2. I read the review paragraph above　Rating

　　　　　　　　　　　　　　　　Total

Friday　　　　　　　**Date**.................................　No. of times daily

1. I read The Scroll Marked V
2. I read the review paragraph above　Rating

　　　　　　　　　　　　　　　　Total

　　　　　　　　　Total points for the week

*Appointments for the week*_____

Monday_____
_____
_____
_____
_____
_____

Tuesday_____
_____
_____
_____
_____
_____

Wednesday_____
_____
_____
_____
_____
_____

Thursday_____
_____
_____
_____
_____
_____

Friday_____
_____
_____
_____
_____

*Achievements of the week*_____
_____
_____
_____
_____
_____
_____

Reflection For The Week

Be such a man, and live such a life, that if every man were such as you, and every life like yours, this earth would be a God's Paradise. —*Phillips Brooks*

Chapter VIII

Do you get moody?

Of course you do. There are days when you'd like to crawl into a hole and just hide from the world. Everything you touch turns to sawdust. You just can't win. You can't make a sale. What's the sense to anything? Right?

And then there are other days when you can do nothing wrong. From the time you awake you're wearing rose colored glasses and enjoying every minute of it. Sales? Completed projects? You can't miss. Everything is going your way.

What causes these fluctuations in our emotional level? We don't know, but some time ago I was fortunate enough to work closely with Professor Edward R. Dewey, head of The Foundation For The Study of Cycles at the University of Pittsburgh. We co-authored a book entitled *"Cycles, The Mysterious Forces That Trigger Events"* (Hawthorn Books).

One of the many cycles we dealt with was the emotional cycle in human beings. Several years ago a scientific study was conducted by Professor Rex Hersey of the University of Pennsylvania. His conclusion was that the emotional cycle in man has an average length of about five weeks. This is the typical length of time it takes for a normal individual to move from one period of elation down the scale to a feeling of worry (the most destructive emotion according to Hersey) and back up again to the next period of elation.

Five weeks! Maybe your emotional cycle is longer or shorter but I'm sure you'll agree that it would be great to know your "high" and "low" periods. Here's a simple method to learn this important secret about yourself. Just prepare a chart similar to the one below:

	Month											
		1	2	3	4	5	6	7	8	9	10	Set up graph for 30 days
Elated	+3											
Happy	+2											
Pleasant feeling	+1											
Neutral	0											
Unpleasant feeling	−1											
Disgusted; sad	−2											
Worried; depressed	−3											

Every evening take a moment to review your general mood of the day. Then place a dot in the box which seems to fit your state of mind for that day. Connect the dots as time goes on.

Soon you will see a pattern forming. This is your natural mood rhythm, and in most cases it will continue.

After a few months you will know, with amazing accuracy, when your next "high" is due and when you should prepare for your next "low." With this knowledge, this ability to predict your future behavior, you will be able to adjust your activities to suit your mood. When you are going through your high period of elation, you will think twice before making rash promises, impossible commitments, or misguided installment purchases. You will also be able to live through your low periods, when nothing is going right, because now you know that this will soon pass.

The Scroll Marked VI wisely reminds you of another fact . . . that your prospect or customer or supervisor or spouse is also going through a mood cycle. You may be "up" . . . but if that other person is "down" you've got a tough road ahead of you . . . yet this should not discourage you. In a few days that individual, now "up" in his mood will be completely receptive to you and your ideas.

Okay, now we know we have moods . . . but we just can't stay home during those "down" weeks or half a year's productivity goes out the window. So what do we do to remain productive even when we're "down?"

For centuries man believed that his thoughts controlled his actions. Then, along came that great psychologist William James who said that "your actions can control your thoughts . . . and your mood." In other words if you act happy you will feel happy . . . if you act enthusiastically you will feel enthusiastic . . . if you act healthy you will feel healthy. You can call it mind-control or any other name you wish . . . but I want to assure you that it works. Yet it remains a deep, dark secret to most salesmen or individuals in every walk of life. Now, you can make every day a great day as you will learn in:

The Scroll Marked VI

Today I will be master of my emotions.

The tides advance; the tides recede. Winter goes and summer comes. Summer wanes and the cold increases. The sun rises; the sun sets. The moon is full; the moon is black. The birds arrive; the birds depart. Flowers bloom; flowers fade. Seeds are sown; harvests are reaped. All nature is a circle of moods and I am a part of nature and so, like the tides, my moods will rise; my moods will fall.

Today I will be master of my emotions.

It is one of nature's tricks, little understood, that each day I awaken with moods that have changed from yesterday. Yesterday's joy will become today's sadness; yet today's sadness will grow into tomorrow's joy. Inside me is a wheel, constantly turning from sadness to joy, from exultation to depression, from happiness to melancholy. Like the flowers, today's full bloom of joy will fade and wither into despondency, yet I will remember that as today's dead flower carries the seed of tomorrow's bloom so, too, does today's sadness carry the seed of tomorrow's joy.

Today I will be master of my emotions.

And how will I master these emotions so that each day

will be productive? For unless my mood is right the day will be a failure. Trees and plants depend on the weather to flourish but I make my own weather, yea I transport it with me. If I bring rain and gloom and darkness and pessimism to my customers then they will react with rain and gloom and darkness and pessimism and they will purchase naught. If I bring my joy and enthusiasm and brightness and laughter to my customers they will react with joy and enthusiasm and brightness and laughter and my weather will produce a harvest of sales and a granary of gold for me.

Today I will be master of my emotions.

And how will I master my emotions so that every day is a happy day, and a productive one? I will learn this secret of the ages: *Weak is he who permits his thoughts to control his actions; strong is he who forces his actions to control his thoughts.* Each day, when I awake, I will follow this plan of battle before I am captured by the forces of sadness, self-pity and failure—

If I feel depressed I will sing.

If I feel sad I will laugh.

If I feel ill I will double my labor.

If I feel fear I will plunge ahead.

If I feel inferior I will wear new garments.

If I feel uncertain I will raise my voice.

If I feel poverty I will think of wealth to come.

If I feel incompetent I will remember past success.

If I feel insignificant I will remember my goals.

Today I will be master of my emotions.

Henceforth, I will know that only those with inferior ability can always be at their best, and I am not inferior. There will be days when I must constantly struggle against forces which would tear me down. Those such as despair and sadness are simple to recognize but there are others which approach with a smile and the hand of friendship and they can also destroy me. Against them, too, I must never relinquish control—

If I become overconfident I will recall my failures.

If I overindulge I will think of past hungers.

If I feel complacency I will remember my competition.

If I enjoy moments of greatness I will remember moments of shame.

If I feel all-powerful I will try to stop the wind.

If I attain great wealth I will remember one unfed mouth.

If I become overly proud I will remember a moment of weakness.

If I feel my skill is unmatched I will look at the stars.

Today I will be master of my emotions.

And with this new knowledge I will also understand and recognize the moods of he on whom I call. I will make allowances for his anger and irritation of today for he knows not the secret of controlling his mind. I can withstand his arrows and insults for now I know that tomorrow he will change and be a joy to approach.

No longer will I judge a man on one meeting; no longer will I fail to call again tomorrow on he who meets me with hate today. This day he will not buy gold chariots for a penny, yet tomorrow he would exchange his home for a tree. My knowledge of this secret will be my key to great wealth.

Today I will be master of my emotions.

Henceforth I will recognize and identify the mystery of moods in all mankind, and in me. From this moment I am prepared to control whatever personality awakes in me each day. I will master my moods through positive action and when I master my moods I will control my destiny.

Today I control my destiny, and my destiny is to become the greatest salesman in the world!

I will become master of myself.

I will become great.

SUCCESS RECORDER
The Twenty-first Week

✻✻✻

Monday   **Date**.............................   No. of times daily

1. I read The Scroll Marked VI
          Review Paragraph for the Week
2. I avoided all negative thoughts of failure and despair by   Rating
   making my actions control my thoughts; I smiled often; I
   moved swiftly; I raised my voice to strengthen my confidence; I made allowances for the moods of others and
   I refused to allow any set-back or problem to discolor
   my day.   Total

                              (Insert number in each box)

Tuesday   **Date**.............................   No. of times daily

1. I read The Scroll Marked VI
2. I read the review paragraph above   Rating

                                                        Total

---

Wednesday   **Date**.............................   No. of times daily

1. I read The Scroll Marked VI
2. I read the review paragraph above   Rating

                                                        Total

---

Thursday   **Date**.............................   No. of times daily

1. I read The Scroll Marked VI
2. I read the review paragraph above   Rating

                                                        Total

---

Friday   **Date**.............................   No. of times daily

1. I read The Scroll Marked VI
2. I read the review paragraph above   Rating

                                                        Total

---

                              Total points for the week

*Appointments for the week*_____

Monday_____
_____
_____
_____
_____
_____

Tuesday_____
_____
_____
_____
_____
_____

Wednesday_____
_____
_____
_____
_____
_____

Thursday_____
_____
_____
_____
_____
_____

Friday_____
_____
_____
_____
_____
_____

*Achievements of the week*_____
_____
_____
_____

Reflection For The Week

If you want to succeed in the world you must make your own opportunities as you go on. The man who waits for some seventh wave to toss him on dry land will find that the seventh wave is a long time a-coming. You can commit no greater folly than to sit by the roadside until someone comes along and invites you to ride with him to wealth or influence. —*John B. Gough*

SUCCESS RECORDER
The Twenty-second Week

❖❖

Monday **Date**................................... No. of times daily

1. I read The Scroll Marked VI
   Review Paragraph for the Week
2. I avoided all negative thoughts of failure and despair by
   making my actions control my thoughts; I smiled often; I
   moved swiftly; I raised my voice to strengthen my confidence; I made allowances for the moods of others and
   I refused to allow any set-back or problem to discolor
   my day.

No. of times daily

Rating

Total

(Insert number in each box)

Tuesday **Date**................................... No. of times daily

1. I read The Scroll Marked VI
2. I read the review paragraph above

Rating

Total

Wednesday **Date**................................... No. of times daily

1. I read The Scroll Marked VI
2. I read the review paragraph above

Rating

Total

Thursday **Date**................................... No. of times daily

1. I read The Scroll Marked VI
2. I read the review paragraph above

Rating

Total

Friday **Date**................................... No. of times daily

1. I read The Scroll Marked VI
2. I read the review paragraph above

Rating

Total

Total points for the week

Appointments for the week _____

Monday _____
_____
_____
_____
_____

Tuesday _____
_____
_____
_____
_____

Wednesday _____
_____
_____
_____
_____

Thursday _____
_____
_____
_____
_____

Friday _____
_____
_____
_____
_____

Achievements of the week _____
_____
_____
_____
_____

Reflection For The Week

The golden moments in the stream of life rush past
us, and we see nothing but sand; the angels come to
visit us, and we only know them when they are gone.

—*George Eliot*

SUCCESS RECORDER
The Twenty-third Week

✿✿✿

Monday   **Date**...............................   No. of times daily

1. I read The Scroll Marked VI
          Review Paragraph for the Week
2. I avoided all negative thoughts of failure and despair by   **Rating**
   making my actions control my thoughts; I smiled often; I
   moved swiftly; I raised my voice to strengthen my confidence; I made allowances for the moods of others and
   I refused to allow any set-back or problem to discolor
   my day.   Total

                              (Insert number in each box)

Tuesday   **Date**...............................   No. of times daily

1. I read The Scroll Marked VI
2. I read the review paragraph above   **Rating**

                                                 Total

Wednesday   **Date**...............................   No. of times daily

1. I read The Scroll Marked VI
2. I read the review paragraph above   **Rating**

                                                 Total

Thursday   **Date**...............................   No. of times daily

1. I read The Scroll Marked VI
2. I read the review paragraph above   **Rating**

                                                 Total

Friday   **Date**...............................   No. of times daily

1. I read The Scroll Marked VI
2. I read the review paragraph above   **Rating**

                                                 Total

                    Total points for the week

*Appointments for the week*_____

Monday_____
_____
_____
_____
_____

Tuesday_____
_____
_____
_____
_____

Wednesday_____
_____
_____
_____
_____

Thursday_____
_____
_____
_____
_____

Friday_____
_____
_____
_____
_____

*Achievements of the week*_____
_____
_____
_____
_____
_____

Reflection For The Week

Everyone has a fair turn to be as great as he pleases.
—Jeremy Collier

SUCCESS RECORDER
The Twenty-fourth Week

❖❖

Monday   **Date**...................   No. of times daily

1. I read The Scroll Marked VI
           Review Paragraph for the Week
2. I avoided all negative thoughts of failure and despair by   Rating
    making my actions control my thoughts; I smiled often; I
    moved swiftly; I raised my voice to strengthen my con-
    fidence; I made allowances for the moods of others and
    I refused to allow any set-back or problem to discolor
    my day.   Total
                        (Insert number in each box)

Tuesday   **Date**...................   No. of times daily

1. I read The Scroll Marked VI
2. I read the review paragraph above   Rating

                                          Total

Wednesday   **Date**...................   No. of times daily

1. I read The Scroll Marked VI
2. I read the review paragraph above   Rating

                                          Total

Thursday   **Date**...................   No. of times daily

1. I read The Scroll Marked VI
2. I read the review paragraph above   Rating

                                          Total

Friday   **Date**...................   No. of times daily

1. I read The Scroll Marked VI
2. I read the review paragraph above   Rating

                                          Total

                              Total points for the week

*Appointments for the week*_____

Monday_____

_____

_____

_____

_____

Tuesday_____

_____

_____

_____

_____

Wednesday_____

_____

_____

_____

_____

Thursday_____

_____

_____

_____

_____

Friday_____

_____

_____

_____

_____

*Achievements of the week*_____

_____

_____

_____

_____

_____

Reflection For The Week

A wise man will make more opportunities than he finds.　　　—*Bacon*

SUCCESS RECORDER
The Twenty-fifth Week

❖❖

Monday Date............................... No. of times daily

1. I read The Scroll Marked VI
       Review Paragraph for the Week

Rating

2. I avoided all negative thoughts of failure and despair by making my actions control my thoughts; I smiled often; I moved swiftly; I raised my voice to strengthen my confidence; I made allowances for the moods of others and I refused to allow any set-back or problem to discolor my day.

Total

(Insert number in each box)

Tuesday Date............................... No. of times daily

1. I read The Scroll Marked VI
2. I read the review paragraph above

Rating

Total

Wednesday Date............................... No. of times daily

1. I read The Scroll Marked VI
2. I read the review paragraph above

Rating

Total

Thursday Date............................... No. of times daily

1. I read The Scroll Marked VI
2. I read the review paragraph above

Rating

Total

Friday Date............................... No. of times daily

1. I read The Scroll Marked VI
2. I read the review paragraph above

Rating

Total

Total points for the week

*Appointments for the week*_____

Monday_____
_____
_____
_____
_____

Tuesday_____
_____
_____
_____
_____

Wednesday_____
_____
_____
_____
_____

Thursday_____
_____
_____
_____
_____

Friday_____
_____
_____
_____
_____

*Achievements of the week*_____
_____
_____
_____
_____

Reflection For The Week

The best men are not those who have waited for chances but who have taken them; besieged the chance; conquered the chance; and made chance their servant.

—*E. H. Chapin*

Chapter IX

Stand on any busy corner and look at faces.

How many are smiling? How many even seem pleased, or happy? We are becoming a nation of frowning robots, rushing like blind ants from place to place, worrying about, well, you name it. I wish we had some statistics on smiles and laughter for I wonder what percentage of us, on any particular day, never laugh or even smile, from the time we rise to the time we retire.

Aren't we foolish . . . as we stagger around with the weight of the world on our shoulders and that frown adding wrinkles where they're not needed? Our somber mood is even killing us. Dr. James Walsh of Fordham University says, "People who laugh actually live longer than those who don't laugh. Few people realize that health actually varies according to the amount of their laughter."

Not only have we forgotten how to laugh, we've forgotten how important it is. Our forefathers who could afford it trotted jesters and buffoons past their dinner table to make them laugh so that their digestion was improved.

Apparently there are a tremendous number of nonlaughers out there because, since *The Greatest Salesman In The World* was published I have probably received more mail concerning The Scroll Marked VII, which you are about to begin reading, than any other, with most of the remarks directed at the scroll's specific injunction to start laughing at yourself.

Sammy Davis was once asked to define success. I'll never forget his answer: "I don't know what success is, but I know what failure is. Failure is trying to please everybody."

If you're trying to please everybody, and you've forgotten how to laugh at others, *and yourself,* now is the time to learn how to say "to heck with it." Stop taking others, and yourself, too seriously. You are a miracle of nature but that doesn't mean you were put here to be a sourpuss, as you will discover in:

The Scroll Marked VII

I will laugh at the world.

No living creature can laugh except man. Trees may bleed when they are wounded, and beasts in the field will cry in pain and hunger, yet only I have the gift of laughter and it is mine to use whenever I choose. Henceforth I will cultivate the habit of laughter.

I will smile and my digestion will improve; I will chuckle and my burdens will be lightened; I will laugh and my life will be lengthened for this is the secret of long life and now it is mine.

I will laugh at the world.

And most of all, I will laugh at myself for man is most comical when he takes himself too seriously. Never will I fall into this trap of the mind. For though I be nature's greatest miracle am I not still a mere grain tossed about by the winds of time? Do I truly know whence I came or whither I am bound? Will my concern for this day not seem foolish ten years hence? Why should I permit the petty happenings of today to disturb me? What can take place before this sun sets which will not seem insignificant in the river of centuries?

I will laugh at the world.

And how can I laugh when confronted with man or deed which offends me so as to bring forth my tears or my curses? Four words I will train myself to say until they become a habit so strong that immediately they will appear in my mind whenever good humor threatens to depart from me. These words, passed down from the ancients, will carry me through every adversity and maintain my life in balance. These four words are: *This too shall pass.*

I will laugh at the world.

For all worldly things shall indeed pass. When I am heavy with heartache I shall console myself that this too shall pass; when I am puffed with success I shall warn myself that this too shall pass. When I am strangled in poverty I shall tell myself that this too shall pass; when I am burdened with wealth I shall tell myself that this too shall pass. Yea, verily, where is he who built the pyramid? Is he not buried within its stone? And will the pyramid, one day, not also be buried under sand? If all things shall pass why should I be of concern for today?

I will laugh at the world.

I will paint this day with laughter; I will frame this night in song. Never will I labor to be happy; rather will I remain too busy to be sad. I will enjoy today's happiness today. It is not grain to be stored in a box. It is not wine to be saved in a jar. It cannot be saved for the morrow. It must be sown and reaped on the same day and this I will do, henceforth.

I will laugh at the world.

And with my laughter all things will be reduced to their proper size. I will laugh at my failures and they will vanish in clouds of new dreams; I will laugh at my successes and they will shrink to their true value. I will laugh at evil and it will die untasted; I will laugh at goodness and it will thrive and abound. Each day will be triumphant only when my smiles bring forth smiles from others and this I do in selfishness, for those on whom I frown are those who purchase not my goods.

I will laugh at the world.

Henceforth will I shed only tears of sweat, for those of sadness or remorse or frustration are of no value in the market place whilst each smile can be exchanged for gold and each kind word, spoken from my heart, can build a castle.

Never will I allow myself to become so important, so wise, so dignified, so powerful, that I forget how to laugh at myself and my world. In this matter I will always remain as a child, for only as a child am I given the ability to look up to another. I will never grow too long for my cot.

I will laugh at the world.

And so long as I can laugh never will I be poor. This then, is one of nature's greatest gifts, and I will waste it no more. Only with laughter and happiness can I truly become a success. Only with laughter and happiness can I enjoy the fruits of my labor. Were it not so, far better would it be to fail, for happiness is the wine that sharpens the taste of the meal. To enjoy success I must have happiness, and laughter will be the maiden who serves me.

I will be happy.

I will be successful.

I will be the greatest salesman the world has ever known.

SUCCESS RECORDER
The Twenty-sixth Week

✤✤✤✤✤✤✤✤✤✤✤✤✤✤✤✤✤✤✤✤✤✤✤✤✤✤✤✤✤✤✤✤✤✤✤✤✤✤✤

Monday   **Date**...............................   No. of times daily

1. I read The Scroll Marked VII
         Review Paragraph for the Week
2. I laughed at the world, and at myself, refusing to take too   Rating
     seriously my petty undertakings; I laughed at my prob-
     lems, my heartaches, my failures . . . even my successes
     and I maintained my perspective by telling myself
     throughout this day, "this too shall pass."   Total

(Insert number in each box)

Tuesday   **Date**...............................   No. of times daily

1. I read The Scroll Marked VII
2. I read the review paragraph above   Rating

                                Total

Wednesday   **Date**...............................   No. of times daily

1. I read The Scroll Marked VII
2. I read the review paragraph above   Rating

                                Total

Thursday   **Date**...............................   No. of times daily

1. I read The Scroll Marked VII
2. I read the review paragraph above   Rating

                                Total

Friday   **Date**...............................   No. of times daily

1. I read The Scroll Marked VII
2. I read the review paragraph above   Rating

                                Total

                        Total points for the week

*Appointments for the week*_____

Monday_____
_____
_____
_____
_____

Tuesday_____
_____
_____
_____
_____

Wednesday_____
_____
_____
_____
_____

Thursday_____
_____
_____
_____
_____

Friday_____
_____
_____
_____
_____

*Achievements of the week*_____
_____
_____
_____
_____
_____
_____

Reflection For The Week

A laugh is worth a hundred groans in any market.

—*Lamb*

SUCCESS RECORDER
The Twenty-seventh Week

✦✦

Monday   **Date**..............................   No. of times daily

1. I read The Scroll Marked VII
       Review Paragraph for the Week
                                                              Rating
2. I laughed at the world, and at myself, refusing to take too
   seriously my petty undertakings; I laughed at my problems, my heartaches, my failures . . . even my successes
   and I maintained my perspective by telling myself   Total
   throughout this day, "this too shall pass."
                          (Insert number in each box)

Tuesday   **Date**..............................   No. of times daily

1. I read The Scroll Marked VII
2. I read the review paragraph above   Rating

                                                  Total

Wednesday   **Date**..............................   No. of times daily

1. I read The Scroll Marked VII
2. I read the review paragraph above   Rating

                                                  Total

Thursday   **Date**..............................   No. of times daily

1. I read The Scroll Marked VII
2. I read the review paragraph above   Rating

                                                  Total

Friday   **Date**..............................   No. of times daily

1. I read The Scroll Marked VII
2. I read the review paragraph above   Rating

                                                  Total

Total points for the week

Appointments for the week _____

Monday _____
_____
_____
_____
_____

Tuesday _____
_____
_____
_____
_____

Wednesday _____
_____
_____
_____
_____

Thursday _____
_____
_____
_____
_____

Friday _____
_____
_____
_____
_____

Achievements of the week _____
_____
_____
_____
_____
_____

Reflection For The Week

If we consider the frequent reliefs we receive from laughter, and how often it breaks the gloom which is apt to depress the mind, one would take care not to grow too wise for so great a pleasure of life.   —*Addison*

SUCCESS RECORDER
The Twenty-eighth Week

❖❖❖

Monday   **Date**................................   No. of times daily

1. I read The Scroll Marked VII
      Review Paragraph for the Week

2. I laughed at the world, and at myself, refusing to take too   **Rating**
seriously my petty undertakings; I laughed at my prob-
lems, my heartaches, my failures . . . even my successes
and I maintained my perspective by telling myself
throughout this day, "this too shall pass."   Total

(Insert number in each box)

Tuesday   **Date**................................   No. of times daily

1. I read The Scroll Marked VII
2. I read the review paragraph above   **Rating**

                                      Total

Wednesday   **Date**................................   No. of times daily

1. I read The Scroll Marked VII
2. I read the review paragraph above   **Rating**

                                      Total

Thursday   **Date**................................   No. of times daily

1. I read The Scroll Marked VII
2. I read the review paragraph above   **Rating**

                                      Total

Friday   **Date**................................   No. of times daily

1. I read The Scroll Marked VII
2. I read the review paragraph above   **Rating**

                                      Total

                         Total points for the week

*Appointments for the week*_____

Monday_____
_____
_____
_____
_____

Tuesday_____
_____
_____
_____
_____

Wednesday_____
_____
_____
_____
_____

Thursday_____
_____
_____
_____
_____

Friday_____
_____
_____
_____
_____

*Achievements of the week*_____
_____
_____
_____
_____
_____

Reflection For The Week

The most utterly lost of all days is that in which you have not once laughed. —*Chamfort*

SUCCESS RECORDER
The Twenty-ninth Week

✳✳✳

Monday　　　　　　　**Date**.................................　　No. of times daily

1. I read The Scroll Marked VII
　　　　Review Paragraph for the Week
2. I laughed at the world, and at myself, refusing to take too
seriously my petty undertakings; I laughed at my problems, my heartaches, my failures . . . even my successes
and I maintained my perspective by telling myself
throughout this day, "this too shall pass."

Rating

Total

(Insert number in each box)

Tuesday　　　　　　　**Date**.................................　　No. of times daily

1. I read The Scroll Marked VII
2. I read the review paragraph above

Rating

Total

Wednesday　　　　　　**Date**.................................　　No. of times daily

1. I read The Scroll Marked VII
2. I read the review paragraph above

Rating

Total

Thursday　　　　　　**Date**.................................　　No. of times daily

1. I read The Scroll Marked VII
2. I read the review paragraph above

Rating

Total

Friday　　　　　　　**Date**.................................　　No. of times daily

1. I read The Scroll Marked VII
2. I read the review paragraph above

Rating

Total

Total points for the week

Appointments for the week _____

Monday _____

_____
_____
_____
_____

Tuesday _____

_____
_____
_____
_____

Wednesday _____

_____
_____
_____
_____

Thursday _____

_____
_____
_____
_____

Friday _____

_____
_____
_____
_____

Achievements of the week _____

_____
_____
_____
_____

Reflection For The Week

I had rather have a fool make me merry, than experience make me sad. —*Shakespeare*

SUCCESS RECORDER
The Thirtieth Week

❉❉

Monday　　　　　　　**Date**............................　　No. of times daily

1. I read The Scroll Marked VII
　　　　Review Paragraph for the Week
2. I laughed at the world, and at myself, refusing to take too
seriously my petty undertakings; I laughed at my problems, my heartaches, my failures . . . even my successes
and I maintained my perspective by telling myself
throughout this day, "this too shall pass."

　　　　　　　(Insert number in each box)

Rating

Total

Tuesday　　　　　　**Date**............................　　No. of times daily

1. I read The Scroll Marked VII
2. I read the review paragraph above

Rating

Total

Wednesday　　　　　**Date**............................　　No. of times daily

1. I read The Scroll Marked VII
2. I read the review paragraph above

Rating

Total

Thursday　　　　　　**Date**............................　　No. of times daily

1. I read The Scroll Marked VII
2. I read the review paragraph above

Rating

Total

Friday　　　　　　　**Date**............................　　No. of times daily

1. I read The Scroll Marked VII
2. I read the review paragraph above

Rating

Total

Total points for the week

*Appointments for the week*_____

Monday_____
_____
_____
_____
_____
_____

Tuesday_____
_____
_____
_____
_____
_____

Wednesday_____
_____
_____
_____
_____
_____

Thursday_____
_____
_____
_____
_____
_____

Friday_____
_____
_____
_____
_____
_____

*Achievements of the week*_____
_____
_____
_____
_____
_____

Reflection For The Week

Be cheerful always. There is no path but will be easier traveled, no load but will be lighter, no shadow on the heart and brain but will lift sooner for a person of determined cheerfulness.　　　　—*Willitts*

Chapter X

Y ou've hung on so well, and you're looking so great! I'm proud of you.

I'm so proud of you that I'm going to let you in on the greatest secret in the world. The president of your company knows it . . . and so does every other individual who ever made it to the top in his own particular career. It really shouldn't be classified as a secret because successful people constantly talk about it openly . . . *but nobody is listening!*

Including you.

Maybe you'll pay attention, now.

The greatest secret in the world is that you only have to be a small, measurable amount better than mediocrity . . . and you've got it made.

Read that again. Burn it into your mind and never forget it.

We live in a world of mediocrity . . . and mediocre individuals. You know it, without taking my word for it. Think of that last new car you bought and how sloppily it was assembled by people who just did their job well enough to get by. And how many things were unfinished in that new house you bought? Remember that jacket with the pockets still sewn together . . . and that magazine you bought with sixteen pages missing?

Charles H. Brower, one of our century's most able and brilliant business executives, put his finger on it all when he said, "We, in America, are living in the high tide of the mediocre, the great era of the goof-off, the age of the job half-done. The land from coast to coast has been enjoying a stampede away from responsibility. It is populated with laundrymen who won't iron shirts, with waiters who won't serve, with carpenters who will come around some day maybe, with executives whose minds are on the golf course, with teachers who demand a single salary schedule so that achievement cannot be rewarded nor poor work punished, with students who take cinch courses because the hard ones make them think, with spiritual delinquents of all kinds who have been triumphantly determined to enjoy what was known until the present crisis as the 'new leisure.'"

You don't have to move ahead to be a success! Just stand fast where you are, doing the best you can, and without your advancing one inch forward you'll be ahead of the pack. Why? Because the others will have all retreated! The struggle was too rough for them. They quit . . . and ran . . . and there you are because there's no one remaining. Mr. Success!

For, as Mr. Brower concluded, "I am a man of great faith. Here and there you see bright minds who are not interested in clockwatching and goofing off. And I would like to say to them, do not be discouraged when you find yourself afloat in a sea of mediocrity. Do not be down-hearted when the tides of foolishness are running high. It is the earnest and devoted few who can turn that tide."

I purposely waited until we were this far along in the book before sharing this secret with you. And I have purposely "buried" it, in the text, so that the casual browser won't find it. Those whom we have lost, along the way, only help to prove the secret they'll never know.

You . . . are something special, and you are worth a fortune to yourself and those you love, if you will only heed the words in:

The Scroll Marked VIII

Today I will multiply my value a hundredfold.

A mulberry leaf touched with the genius of man becomes silk.

A field of clay touched with the genius of man becomes a castle.

A cyprus tree touched with the genius of man becomes a shrine.

A cut of sheep's hair touched with the genius of man becomes raiment for a king.

If it is possible for leaves and clay and wood and hair to have their value multiplied a hundred, yea a thousandfold by man, cannot I do the same with clay which bears my name?

Today I will multiply my value a hundredfold.

THE GREATEST SECRET IN THE WORLD

I am liken to a grain of wheat which faces one of three futures. The wheat can be placed in a sack and dumped in a stall until it is fed to swine. Or it can be ground to flour and made into bread. Or it can be placed in the earth and allowed to grow until its golden head divides and produces a thousand grains from the one.

I am liken to a grain of wheat with one difference. The wheat cannot choose whether it be fed to swine, ground for bread, or planted to multiply. I have a choice and I will not let my life be fed to swine nor will I let it be ground under the rocks of failure and despair to be broken open and devoured by the will of others.

Today I will multiply my value a hundredfold.

To grow and multiply it is necessary to plant the wheat grain in the darkness of the earth and my failures, my despairs, my ignorance, and my inabilities are the darkness in which I have been planted in order to ripen. Now, like the wheat grain which will sprout and blossom only if it is nurtured with rain and sun and warm winds, I too must nurture my body and mind to fulfill my dreams. But to grow to full stature the wheat must wait on the whims of nature. I need not wait for I have the power to choose my own destiny.

Today I will multiply my value a hundredfold.

And how will I accomplish this? First I will set goals for the day, the week, the month, the year, and my life. Just as the rain must fall before the wheat will crack its shell and sprout, so must I have objectives before my life will crystallize. In setting my goals I will consider my best performance of the past and multiply it a hundredfold. This will be the standard by which I will live in the future. Never will I be of concern that my goals are too high for is it not better to aim my spear at the moon and strike only an eagle than to aim my spear at the eagle and strike only a rock?

Today I will multiply my value a hundredfold.

The height of my goals will not hold me in awe though I may stumble often before they are reached. If I stumble I will rise and my falls will not concern me for all men must stumble often to reach the hearth. Only a worm is free from the worry of stumbling. I am not a worm. I am not an onion plant. I am not a sheep. I am a man. Let others build a cave with their clay. I will build a castle with mine.

Today I will multiply my value a hundredfold.

And just as the sun must warm the earth to bring forth the seedling of wheat so, too, will the words on these scrolls warm my life and turn my dreams into reality. Today I will surpass every action which I performed yesterday. I will climb today's mountain to the utmost of my ability yet tomorrow I will climb higher than today, and the next will be higher than tomorrow. To surpass the deeds of others is unimportant; to surpass my own deeds is all.

Today I will multiply my value a hundredfold.

And just as the warm wind guides the wheat to maturity, the same winds will carry my voice to those who will listen and my words will announce my goals. Once spoken I dare not recall them lest I lose face. I will be as my own prophet and though all may laugh at my utterances they will hear my plans, they will know my dreams; and thus there will be no escape for me until my words become accomplished deeds.

Today I will multiply my value a hundredfold.

I will commit not the terrible crime of aiming too low.

I will do the work that a failure will not do.

I will always let my reach exceed my grasp.

I will never be content with my performance in the market.

I will always raise my goals as soon as they are attained.

I will always strive to make the next hour better than this one.

I will always announce my goals to the world.

Yet, never will I proclaim my accomplishments. Let the world, instead, approach me with praise and may I have the wisdom to receive it in humility.

Today I will multiply my value a hundredfold.

One grain of wheat when multiplied a hundredfold will produce a hundred stalks. Multiply these a hundredfold, ten times, and they will feed all the cities of the earth, Am I not more than a grain of wheat?

Today I will multiply my value a hundredfold.

And when it is done I will do it again, and again, and there will be astonishment and wonder at my greatness as the words of these scrolls are fulfilled in me.

SUCCESS RECORDER
The Thirty-first Week

❖❖

Monday   **Date**.......................   No. of times daily

1. I read The Scroll Marked VIII
              Review Paragraph for the Week
2. I set goals for today that were double my productivity of   Rating
    yesterday; I put myself "on the spot" by announcing
    those goals to all; I attempted at least one task which I
    would have avoided like the plague yesterday and I am
    still not content with this day's performance.   Total
                                (Insert number in each box)

Tuesday   **Date**.......................   No. of times daily

1. I read The Scroll Marked VIII
2. I read the review paragraph above   Rating

                                                   Total

Wednesday   **Date**.......................   No. of times daily

1. I read The Scroll Marked VIII
2. I read the review paragraph above   Rating

                                                   Total

Thursday   **Date**.......................   No. of times daily

1. I read The Scroll Marked VIII
2. I read the review paragraph above   Rating

                                                   Total

Friday   **Date**.......................   No. of times daily

1. I read The Scroll Marked VIII
2. I read the review paragraph above   Rating

                                                   Total

                          Total points for the week

*Appointments for the week*_____

Monday_____
_____
_____
_____
_____

Tuesday_____
_____
_____
_____
_____

Wednesday_____
_____
_____
_____
_____

Thursday_____
_____
_____
_____
_____

Friday_____
_____
_____
_____
_____

*Achievements of the week*_____
_____
_____
_____
_____
_____

Reflection For The Week

Mediocrity is excellent to the eyes of mediocre people.

—*Joubert*

SUCCESS RECORDER
The Thirty-second Week

❖❖

Monday **Date**................................... No. of times daily

1. I read The Scroll Marked VIII
   Review Paragraph for the Week
2. I set goals for today that were double my productivity of   Rating
   yesterday; I put myself "on the spot" by announcing
   those goals to all; I attempted at least one task which I
   would have avoided like the plague yesterday and I am
   still not content with this day's performance.   Total
   (Insert number in each box)

Tuesday **Date**................................... No. of times daily

1. I read The Scroll Marked VIII
2. I read the review paragraph above   Rating

   Total

Wednesday **Date**................................... No. of times daily

1. I read The Scroll Marked VIII
2. I read the review paragraph above   Rating

   Total

Thursday **Date**................................... No. of times daily

1. I read The Scroll Marked VIII
2. I read the review paragraph above   Rating

   Total

Friday **Date**................................... No. of times daily

1. I read The Scroll Marked VIII
2. I read the review paragraph above   Rating

   Total

Total points for the week

*Appointments for the week*_____

Monday_____
_____
_____
_____
_____

Tuesday_____
_____
_____
_____
_____

Wednesday_____
_____
_____
_____
_____

Thursday_____
_____
_____
_____
_____

Friday_____
_____
_____
_____
_____

*Achievements of the week*_____
_____
_____
_____
_____

Reflection For The Week

The highest order of mind is accused of folly, as well as the lowest. Nothing is thoroughly approved but mediocrity. The majority has established this, and it fixes its fangs on whatever gets beyond it either way.

—*Pascal*

SUCCESS RECORDER
The Thirty-third Week

❖❖

Monday   **Date**....................   No. of times daily

1. I read The Scroll Marked VIII
          Review Paragraph for the Week
2. I set goals for today that were double my productivity of   Rating
   yesterday; I put myself "on the spot" by announcing
   those goals to all; I attempted at least one task which I
   would have avoided like the plague yesterday and I am
   still not content with this day's performance.   Total
                      (Insert number in each box)

Tuesday   **Date**....................   No. of times daily

1. I read The Scroll Marked VIII
2. I read the review paragraph above   Rating

                                        Total

Wednesday   **Date**....................   No. of times daily

1. I read The Scroll Marked VIII
2. I read the review paragraph above   Rating

                                        Total

Thursday   **Date**....................   No. of times daily

1. I read The Scroll Marked VIII
2. I read the review paragraph above   Rating

                                        Total

Friday   **Date**....................   No. of times daily

1. I read The Scroll Marked VIII
2. I read the review paragraph above   Rating

                                        Total

                    Total points for the week

Appointments for the week _____

Monday _____

_____
_____
_____
_____

Tuesday _____

_____
_____
_____
_____

Wednesday _____

_____
_____
_____
_____

Thursday _____

_____
_____
_____
_____

Friday _____

_____
_____
_____
_____

Achievements of the week _____

_____
_____
_____
_____
_____

Reflection For The Week

Folks who never do any more than they get paid for,
never get paid for any more than they do. —*Elbert Hubbard*

SUCCESS RECORDER
The Thirty-fourth Week

❖❖

Monday   **Date**........................   No. of times daily

1. I read The Scroll Marked VIII
          Review Paragraph for the Week

2. I set goals for today that were double my productivity of   Rating
    yesterday; I put myself "on the spot" by announcing
    those goals to all; I attempted at least one task which I
    would have avoided like the plague yesterday and I am
    still not content with this day's performance.   Total

(Insert number in each box)

Tuesday   **Date**........................   No. of times daily

1. I read The Scroll Marked VIII
2. I read the review paragraph above   Rating

                                        Total

Wednesday   **Date**........................   No. of times daily

1. I read The Scroll Marked VIII
2. I read the review paragraph above   Rating

                                        Total

Thursday   **Date**........................   No. of times daily

1. I read The Scroll Marked VIII
2. I read the review paragraph above   Rating

                                        Total

Friday   **Date**........................   No. of times daily

1. I read The Scroll Marked VIII
2. I read the review paragraph above   Rating

                                        Total

                    Total points for the week

*Appointments for the week*_____

Monday_____

_____
_____
_____
_____

Tuesday_____

_____
_____
_____
_____

Wednesday_____

_____
_____
_____
_____

Thursday_____

_____
_____
_____
_____

Friday_____

_____
_____
_____
_____

*Achievements of the week*_____

_____
_____
_____
_____
_____

Reflection For The Week

Those who attain to any excellence commonly spend life in some one single pursuit, for excellence is not often gained upon easier terms.   —*Johnson*

SUCCESS RECORDER

The Thirty-fifth Week

****

Monday **Date**.................................... No. of times daily

1. I read The Scroll Marked VIII ☐

Review Paragraph for the Week

2. I set goals for today that were double my productivity of yesterday; I put myself "on the spot" by announcing those goals to all; I attempted at least one task which I would have avoided like the plague yesterday and I am still not content with this day's performance. Rating ☐

(Insert number in each box) Total ☐

Tuesday **Date**.................................... No. of times daily

1. I read The Scroll Marked VIII ☐
2. I read the review paragraph above Rating ☐

Total ☐

Wednesday **Date**.................................... No. of times daily

1. I read The Scroll Marked VIII ☐
2. I read the review paragraph above Rating ☐

Total ☐

Thursday **Date**.................................... No. of times daily

1. I read The Scroll Marked VIII ☐
2. I read the review paragraph above Rating ☐

Total ☐

Friday **Date**.................................... No. of times daily

1. I read The Scroll Marked VIII ☐
2. I read the review paragraph above Rating ☐

Total ☐

Total points for the week ☐

*Appointments for the week*_____

Monday_____
_____
_____
_____
_____

Tuesday_____
_____
_____
_____
_____

Wednesday_____
_____
_____
_____
_____

Thursday_____
_____
_____
_____
_____

Friday_____
_____
_____
_____
_____

*Achievements of the week*_____
_____
_____
_____
_____
_____

Reflection For The Week

Great souls have wills; feeble ones have only wishes.
—Chinese Proverb

Chapter XI

Some very brilliant individuals at our National Bureau of Standards have been telling us that this still beautiful earth on which we all perform is slowing down in its daily rotation. Eventually, they claim, this will produce a twenty-five hour day . . . 1,800,000 *centuries* from now!

But you can't wait until then for that extra bonus hour to sell or produce more goods for a higher income . . . and in truth, how much of this day's 23 hours, 56 minutes, 4.09 seconds do you use wisely?

George Severance, who represents the Ohio National Life Insurance Company, is one of the most outstanding and productive salesmen in the entire insurance industry . . . now. But there were leaner and almost desperate days before he took stock of himself, as he disclosed to W. Clement Stone in an article for Success Unlimited:

"One day the total amount of my debts struck me like a bolt of lightning. I was faced with a real financial crisis. Then I recalled a statement I had read somewhere, 'Don't expect what you don't expect.'"

George decided to keep a record of how he spent his time, every salesman's greatest asset. "I found that I had been spending as much as 32 hours in a single month drinking coffee with my friends. I was amazed, for I realized that this was equivalent to four working days. And then I realized that my lunch hours were sometimes a full hour longer than they should have been."

Just as you are using your Success Recorder as a means of self-examining how you perform daily regarding one specific success principle, George developed what he called a Social Time Recorder so that he could account, to himself, for his productive and non-productive time each day.

"When I looked back, I found that in many respects I was a social success during business hours. But when I developed my Social Time Recorder, I realized:

'If a business day is a social success, it has been a business failure.'"

The italics in the above statement are mine. If I could convince my publisher to print that statement in 32-point Day-glow letters I'd do it . . . for I want you never to forget what you have just read:

"If a business day is a social success, it has been a business failure."

Why is it easier to make any day a social success than a business success? You know the answer . . . because you've been there. I've been there. Socializing is easy, it's fun. Selling, working, doing the things that are difficult to do, is rough and not fun. So, like the rest of nature which also follows the line of least resistance we procrastinate, we stall, we make innumerable excuses to avoid what we *know* should be done.

We avoid getting into action, productive action, as long as possible, and if there is any single identifying characteristic of those 95% who have settled for a life of mediocrity it is this trait of inactivity.

But that's not for you. You've come too far to let this bad habit defeat you. Procrastination can be driven from your personality through the simple technique of constantly commanding yourself to get into action . . . and then obeying that command immediately. You begin your basic training on this bad habit with little acts such as:

You walk across your living room rug. On the rug is a piece of torn paper. The "old you" would leave it for your wife to attend to when she cleans the room. The "new you" picks it up, *now*.

You pull your automobile out of the garage in the morning. The city's rubbish pick-up service has already come by and emptied your two containers. The "old you" would leave them in the driveway until you returned from work that evening before putting them back in the garage. The "new you" puts them back, *now*.

The "old you" reviews his morning mail and then answers only those memos and letters which absolutely must be handled and puts the rest aside for later. The "new you," knowing how much time can be saved by handling every piece of correspondence only once, answers every piece, *now*.

The "old you" gets a pain, of one sort or another, in your chest, and resolves to go to a doctor, some day when you're not so "busy." The "new you" goes, *now*.

(That "some day" for the "old you" might never come!)

I'm reasonably certain that you could fill many pages with the things you do that fit into this "put-off" category. Yet, if you cannot overcome this vice then all the time you have put into your Success Recorder has been wasted and we've both got too much invested in you to let that happen.

So let's get into action! Let's begin reading!

The Scroll Marked IX

My dreams are worthless, my plans are dust, my goals are impossible.

All are of no value unless they are followed by action. I will act now.

Never has there been a map, however carefully executed to detail and scale, which carried its owner over even one inch of ground. Never has there been a parchment of law, however fair, which prevented one crime. Never has there been a scroll, even such as the one I hold, which earned so much as a penny or produced a single word of acclamation. Action, alone, is the tinder which ignites the map, the parchment, this scroll, my dreams, my plans, my goals, into a living force. Action is the food and drink which will nourish my success.

I will act now.

My procrastination which has held me back was born of fear and now I recognize this secret mined from the depths of all courageous hearts. Now I know that to conquer fear I must always act without hesitation and the flutters in my heart will vanish. Now I know that action reduces the lion of terror to an ant of equanimity.

I will act now.

Henceforth, I will remember the lesson of the firefly who gives off its light only when it is on the wing, only when it is in action. I will become a firefly and even in the day my glow will be seen in spite of the sun. Let others be as butterflies who preen their wings yet depend on the charity of a flower for life. I will be as the firefly and my light will brighten the world.

I will act now.

I will not avoid the tasks of today and charge them to tomorrow for I know that tomorrow never comes. Let me act now even though my actions may not bring happiness or success for it is better to act and fail than not to act and flounder. Happiness, in truth, may not be the fruit plucked by my action yet without action all fruit will die on the vine.

I will act now.

I will act now. I will act now. I will act now. Henceforth, I will repeat these words again and again and again, each hour, each day, every day, until the words became as much a habit as my breathing and the actions which follow become as instinctive as the blinking of my eyelids. With these words I can condition my mind to perform every act necessary for my success. With these words I can condition my mind to meet every challenge which the failure avoids.

I will act now.

I will repeat these words again and again and again.

When I awake I will say them and leap from my cot while the failure sleeps yet another hour.

I will act now.

When I enter the market place I will say them and immediately confront my first prospect while the failure ponders yet his possibility of rebuff.

I will act now.

When I face a closed door I will say them and knock while the failure waits outside with fear and trepidation.

I will act now.

When I face the temptation I will say them and immediately act to remove myself from evil.

I will act now.

When I am tempted to quit and begin again tomorrow I will say them and immediately act to consummate another sale.

I will act now.

Only action determines my value in the market place and to multiply my value I will multiply my actions. I will walk where the failure fears to walk. I will work when the failure seeks rest. I will talk when the failure remains silent. I will call on ten who can buy my goods while the failure makes grand plans to call on one. I will say it is done before the failure says it is too late.

I will act now.

For now is all I have. Tomorrow is the day reserved for the labor of the lazy. I am not lazy. Tomorrow is the day when the evil become good. I am not evil. Tomorrow is the day when the weak become strong. I am not weak. Tomorrow is the day when the failure will succeed. I am not a failure.

I will act now.

When the lion is hungry he eats. When the eagle has thirst he drinks. Lest they act, both will perish.

I hunger for success. I thirst for happiness and peace of mind. Lest I act I will perish in a life of failure, misery, and sleepless nights.

THE GREATEST SECRET IN THE WORLD

I will command, and I will obey mine own command.

I will act now.

Success will not wait. If I delay she will become betrothed to another and lost to me forever.

This is the time. This is the place. I am the man.

I will act now.

SUCCESS RECORDER
The Thirty-sixth Week

✦✦

Monday   **Date**.............................   No. of times daily

1. I read The Scroll Marked IX
        Review Paragraph for the Week
2. I got into action from the time I awoke; I leaped quickly   Rating
   from my bed; I repeated to myself throughout the day,
   "Act now, now, now!"; I overcame my fears through action; I put off no distasteful chore for another time; I
   moved swiftly from prospect to prospect or from project
   to project and I moved fast to avoid temptations. Today
   I was in action!   Total

   (Insert number in each box)

Tuesday   **Date**.............................   No. of times daily

1. I read The Scroll Marked IX
2. I read the review paragraph above   Rating

          Total

Wednesday   **Date**.............................   No. of times daily

1. I read The Scroll Marked IX
2. I read the review paragraph above   Rating

          Total

Thursday   **Date**.............................   No. of times daily

1. I read The Scroll Marked IX
2. I read the review paragraph above   Rating

          Total

Friday   **Date**.............................   No. of times daily

1. I read The Scroll Marked IX
2. I read the review paragraph above   Rating

          Total

          Total points for the week

Appointments for the week

Monday

Tuesday

Wednesday

Thursday

Friday

Achievements of the week

Reflection For The Week

Heaven never helps the man who will not act.

—*Sophocles*

SUCCESS RECORDER
The Thirty-seventh Week

❖❖❖

Monday   **Date**.............................   No. of times daily

1. I read The Scroll Marked IX
   Review Paragraph for the Week
2. I got into action from the time I awoke; I leaped quickly   Rating
   from my bed; I repeated to myself throughout the day,
   "Act now, now, now!"; I overcame my fears through action; I put off no distasteful chore for another time; I
   moved swiftly from prospect to prospect or from project
   to project and I moved fast to avoid temptations. Today
   I was in action!   Total

(Insert number in each box)

Tuesday   **Date**.............................   No. of times daily

1. I read The Scroll Marked IX
2. I read the review paragraph above   Rating

                                        Total

Wednesday   **Date**.............................   No. of times daily

1. I read The Scroll Marked IX
2. I read the review paragraph above   Rating

                                        Total

Thursday   **Date**.............................   No. of times daily

1. I read The Scroll Marked IX
2. I read the review paragraph above   Rating

                                        Total

Friday   **Date**.............................   No. of times daily

1. I read The Scroll Marked IX
2. I read the review paragraph above   Rating

                                        Total

Total points for the week

Appointments for the week_____

Monday_____

_____
_____
_____
_____

Tuesday_____

_____
_____
_____
_____

Wednesday_____

_____
_____
_____
_____

Thursday_____

_____
_____
_____
_____

Friday_____

_____
_____
_____
_____

Achievements of the week_____

_____
_____
_____
_____
_____

Reflection For The Week

I have never heard anything about the resolutions of
the apostles, but a good deal about their acts.

—Horace Mann

SUCCESS RECORDER
The Thirty-eighth Week

✦✦

Monday　　　　　　　**Date**................................　　No. of times daily

1. I read The Scroll Marked IX
　　　　　Review Paragraph for the Week
2. I got into action from the time I awoke; I leaped quickly　　Rating
from my bed; I repeated to myself throughout the day,
"Act now, now, now!"; I overcame my fears through action; I put off no distasteful chore for another time; I
moved swiftly from prospect to prospect or from project
to project and I moved fast to avoid temptations. Today
I was in action!　　　　　　　　　　　　　　　　　　Total

(Insert number in each box)

Tuesday　　　　　　　**Date**................................　　No. of times daily

1. I read The Scroll Marked IX
2. I read the review paragraph above　　　　　　　　Rating

　　　　　　　　　　　　　　　　　　　　Total

Wednesday　　　　　　**Date**................................　　No. of times daily

1. I read The Scroll Marked IX
2. I read the review paragraph above　　　　　　　　Rating

　　　　　　　　　　　　　　　　　　　　Total

Thursday　　　　　　　**Date**................................　　No. of times daily

1. I read The Scroll Marked IX
2. I read the review paragraph above　　　　　　　　Rating

　　　　　　　　　　　　　　　　　　　　Total

Friday　　　　　　　　**Date**................................　　No. of times daily

1. I read The Scroll Marked IX
2. I read the review paragraph above　　　　　　　　Rating

　　　　　　　　　　　　　　　　　　　　Total

　　　　　　　　　　　　Total points for the week

*Appointments for the week*_____

Monday_____

_____

_____

_____

_____

Tuesday_____

_____

_____

_____

_____

Wednesday_____

_____

_____

_____

_____

Thursday_____

_____

_____

_____

_____

Friday_____

_____

_____

_____

_____

*Achievements of the week*_____

_____

_____

_____

_____

_____

_____

Reflection For The Week

Good thoughts, though God accept them, yet toward men are little better than good dreams except they be put in action.   —*Bacon*

SUCCESS RECORDER
The Thirty-ninth Week

❖❖

Monday   **Date**................................   No. of times daily

1. I read The Scroll Marked IX
         Review Paragraph for the Week
2. I got into action from the time I awoke; I leaped quickly   Rating
   from my bed; I repeated to myself throughout the day,
   "Act now, now, now!"; I overcame my fears through action; I put off no distasteful chore for another time; I
   moved swiftly from prospect to prospect or from project
   to project and I moved fast to avoid temptations. Today
   I was in action!   Total

                        (Insert number in each box)

Tuesday   **Date**................................   No. of times daily

1. I read The Scroll Marked IX
2. I read the review paragraph above   Rating

                                                          Total

---

Wednesday   **Date**................................   No. of times daily

1. I read The Scroll Marked IX
2. I read the review paragraph above   Rating

                                                          Total

---

Thursday   **Date**................................   No. of times daily

1. I read The Scroll Marked IX
2. I read the review paragraph above   Rating

                                                          Total

---

Friday   **Date**................................   No. of times daily

1. I read The Scroll Marked IX
2. I read the review paragraph above   Rating

                                                          Total

---

                        Total points for the week

Appointments for the week _____

Monday _____
_____
_____
_____
_____

Tuesday _____
_____
_____
_____
_____

Wednesday _____
_____
_____
_____
_____

Thursday _____
_____
_____
_____
_____

Friday _____
_____
_____
_____
_____

Achievements of the week _____
_____
_____
_____
_____
_____

Reflection For The Week

Life was not given for indolent contemplation and
study of self; nor for brooding over emotions of piety;
actions and actions only determine the worth.   —*Fichte*

SUCCESS RECORDER
The Fortieth Week

❖❖❖

Monday   **Date**..........................   No. of times daily

1. I read The Scroll Marked IX
            Review Paragraph for the Week
2. I got into action from the time I awoke; I leaped quickly   Rating
   from my bed; I repeated to myself throughout the day,
   "Act now, now, now!"; I overcame my fears through action; I put off no distasteful chore for another time; I
   moved swiftly from prospect to prospect or from project
   to project and I moved fast to avoid temptations. Today
   I was in action!   Total

                              (Insert number in each box)

Tuesday   **Date**..........................   No. of times daily

1. I read The Scroll Marked IX
2. I read the review paragraph above   Rating

                                                    Total

Wednesday   **Date**..........................   No. of times daily

1. I read The Scroll Marked IX
2. I read the review paragraph above   Rating

                                                    Total

Thursday   **Date**..........................   No. of times daily

1. I read The Scroll Marked IX
2. I read the review paragraph above   Rating

                                                    Total

Friday   **Date**..........................   No. of times daily

1. I read The Scroll Marked IX
2. I read the review paragraph above   Rating

                                                    Total

                              Total points for the week

*Appointments for the week*_____

Monday_____
_____
_____
_____
_____

Tuesday_____
_____
_____
_____
_____

Wednesday_____
_____
_____
_____
_____

Thursday_____
_____
_____
_____
_____

Friday_____
_____
_____
_____
_____

*Achievements of the week*_____
_____
_____
_____
_____
_____

Reflection For The Week

Our grand business is not to see what lies dimly at a
distance, but to do what lies clearly at hand.   —*Carlyle*

Chapter XII

$\mathbf{D}$oes God exist?

If you're positive he does not . . . then you can skip these last five weeks of your Success Recorder . . . because The Scroll Marked X deals with a prayer and there's not much sense praying if you don't believe that anyone is listening.

In 1958, as their contribution to honor the International Geophysical Year, G. P. Putnam's Sons published a book entitled *The Evidence of God in an Expanding Universe*. For anyone who has doubted, at one time or another, that there is a Power beyond any we know (and who of us have perfect faith?) I strongly urge you to find a copy and read it.

In its pages you will meet not one religious leader or Biblical expert. Instead, forty men of science, each with his own long record of accomplishments and honors, presents his scientific reasons for believing that there is a God.

I was amazed then, and still am today, that this learned group of men would expose their personal beliefs to ridicule from so many of their scientific peers whose philosophy is usually one of atheistic materialism and whose only god is modern technical achievement.

Yet, there they were, men like biophysicist Frank Allen, zoologist Edward Luther Kessel, physiologist Walter Oscar Lundberg, mathematician and physicist Donald Henry Porter, geneticist John William Klotz, geochemist Donald Robert Carr, astronomer Peter W. Stoner, chemical engineer Olin Carroll Karkalits, medical internist Malcolm Duncan Winter, Jr., biologist Cecil Boyce Hamann, research chemist Edmund Carl Kornfield, soil scientist Lester John Zimmerman and twenty-eight other creative scientists. And each presented logic and reason for the existence of God from his own field of science which did more to buttress my wavering faith than all the sermons I had ever heard.

I'm going to assume, although assuming anything is a good way to get into trouble, that you do believe in a Power or force which does have some control over your life and although you might have done very little to maintain "lines of communication" in recent years you still believe that there is "something there." That's all I ask.

I will not dare hope that I can touch you as much as a famous surgeon once was affected by a little girl on whom he was about to operate. As he was about to place her on the operating table he said, "Before we can make you well we must put you to sleep."

She smiled up at him and said, "If you are going to put me to sleep I must say my prayers first." And with that she jumped from the table, knelt on the marble floor and prayed, "Now I lay me down to sleep . . ."

Later, the surgeon said that he prayed that night for the first time since he was a child.

During the next five weeks (and hopefully forever after) you are not going to pray for help or personal gain of any sort . . . only for guidance. Did you know that in Washington, D.C., hundreds of our lawmakers meet each week in private prayer breakfasts which end with these powerful individuals on their knees seeking divine guidance?

Can you picture generals, admirals, cabinet members, senators, representatives, White House staff members, individuals with the most powerful positions in the most powerful country in the world . . . on their knees . . . in a spirit of helpless humility . . . praying?

Can you picture that two-hundred pound, six feet three, rugged and handsome Senator Harold Hughes of Iowa, wearing a wrist watch containing the twelve letters JUST FOR TODAY instead of numbers, fall to his knees after conducting a seminar for visiting foreign dignitaries and educators . . . and leading them in prayer?

Do they know something we don't know?

Perhaps. And what they know is that they can't "hack it" alone. But they never ask for favors or petty victories . . . only for the guidance which will enable them to make their own choice to resolve their problems and challenges of the day.

It is my belief that prayers uttered for personal gain or to resolve some crisis in your life fall on deaf ears like the man and his son who were plowing their field in Georgia when a terrible lightning storm erupted. The man ran for the farmhouse, looked back and saw his son staring skyward.

"Hey," he yelled, "what in tarnation you doin'?"

"I'm prayin', Dad."

"Prayin'! A scared prayer ain't worth a damn, Son—run!"

The Salesman's Prayer, in the final scroll, is an ideal finale for all the weeks you have labored so long to keep your Success Recorder. In its text you will find a review of all the success principles which you have concentrated on, individually, to improve your life.

And through it, you, I know, will find the strength and the inspiration to continue moving forward no matter what fate has in store for you.

Remember, *"Failure will never overtake you if your determination to succeed is strong enough."*

Have a happy and beautiful five weeks with:

The Scroll Marked X

Who is of so little faith that in a moment of great disaster or heartbreak has not called to his God? Who has not cried out when confronted with danger, death, or mystery beyond his normal experience or comprehension? From where has this deep instinct come which escapes from the mouth of all living creatures in moments of peril?

Move your hand in haste before another's eyes and his eyelids will blink. Tap another on his knee and his leg will jump. Confront another with dark horror and his mouth will say, "My God" from the same deep impulse.

My life need not be filled with religion in order for me to recognize this greatest mystery of nature. All creatures that walk the earth, including man, possess the instinct to cry for help. Why do we possess this instinct, this gift?

Are not our cries a form of prayer? Is it not incomprehensible in a world governed by nature's law to give a lamb, or a mule, or a bird, or man the instinct to cry out for help lest some great mind has also provided that the cry should be heard by some superior power having the ability to hear and to answer our cry? Henceforth I will pray, but my cries for help will only be cries for guidance.

Never will I pray for the material things of the world. I am not calling to a servant to bring me food. I am not ordering an innkeeper to provide me with room. Never will I seek delivery of gold, love, good health, petty victories, fame, success, or happiness. Only for guidance will I pray, that I may be shown the way to acquire these things, and my prayer will always be answered.

The guidance I seek may come, or the guidance I seek may not come, but are not both of these an answer? If a child seeks bread from his father and it is not forthcoming has not the father answered?

I will pray for guidance, and I will pray as a salesman, in this manner—

Oh creator of all things, help me. For this day I go out into the world naked and alone, and without your hand to guide me I will wander far from the path which leads to success and happiness.

THE GREATEST SECRET IN THE WORLD

I ask not for gold or garments or even opportunities equal to my ability; instead, guide me so that I may acquire ability equal to my opportunities.

You have taught the lion and the eagle how to hunt and prosper with teeth and claw. Teach me how to hunt with words and prosper with love so that I may be a lion among men and an eagle in the market place.

Help me to remain humble through obstacles and failures; yet hide not from mine eyes the prize that will come with victory.

Assign me tasks to which others have failed; yet guide me to pluck the seeds of success from their failures. Confront me with fears that will temper my spirit; yet endow me with courage to laugh at my misgivings.

Spare me sufficient days to reach my goals; yet help me to live this day as though it be my last.

Guide me in my words that they may bear fruit; yet silence me from gossip that none be maligned.

Discipline me in the habit of trying and trying again; yet show me the way to make use of the law of averages. Favor me with alertness to recognize opportunity; yet endow me with patience which will concentrate my strength.

Bathe me in good habits that the bad ones may drown; yet

grant me compassion for weaknesses in others. Suffer me to know that all things shall pass; yet help me to count my blessings of today.

Expose me to hate so it not be a stranger; yet fill my cup with love to turn strangers into friends.

But all these things be only if thy will. I am a small and a lonely grape clutching the vine yet thou hast made me different from all others. Verily, there must be a special place for me. Guide me. Help me. Show me the way.

Let me become all you planned for me when my seed was planted and selected by you to sprout in the vineyard of the world.

Help this humble salesman.
Guide me, God.

SUCCESS RECORDER
The Forty-first Week

❖❖❖

Monday   **Date**.............................   No. of times daily

1. I read The Scroll Marked X
          Review Paragraph for the Week
2. I prayed today; I repeated The Salesman's Prayer as part   Rating
    of the scroll but I also spoke a few words of my own, ask-
    ing for guidance in my personal and business problems
    and thanking my Creator for giving me the privilege of
    making something of this day . . . and my life.   Total
                         (Insert number in each box)

Tuesday   **Date**.............................   No. of times daily

1. I read The Scroll Marked X
2. I read the review paragraph above   Rating

                                                  Total

Wednesday   **Date**.............................   No. of times daily

1. I read The Scroll Marked X
2. I read the review paragraph above   Rating

                                                  Total

Thursday   **Date**.............................   No. of times daily

1. I read The Scroll Marked X
2. I read the review paragraph above   Rating

                                                  Total

Friday   **Date**.............................   No. of times daily

1. I read The Scroll Marked X
2. I read the review paragraph above   Rating

                                                  Total

                         Total points for the week

*Appointments for the week*_____

Monday_____
_____
_____
_____
_____
_____

Tuesday_____
_____
_____
_____
_____
_____

Wednesday_____
_____
_____
_____
_____
_____

Thursday_____
_____
_____
_____
_____
_____

Friday_____
_____
_____
_____
_____
_____

*Achievements of the week*_____
_____
_____
_____
_____
_____

Reflection For The Week

I have been driven many times to my knees by the overwhelming conviction that I had nowhere to go. My own wisdom, and that of all about me, seemed insufficient for the day.   —*Abraham Lincoln*

SUCCESS RECORDER
The Forty-second Week

❖❖❖

Monday   **Date** ....   No. of times daily

1. I read The Scroll Marked X
   Review Paragraph for the Week
2. I prayed today; I repeated The Salesman's Prayer as part   Rating
   of the scroll but I also spoke a few words of my own, ask-
   ing for guidance in my personal and business problems
   and thanking my Creator for giving me the privilege of
   making something of this day . . . and my life.   Total

   (Insert number in each box)

Tuesday   **Date** ....   No. of times daily

1. I read The Scroll Marked X
2. I read the review paragraph above   Rating

                        Total

Wednesday   **Date** ....   No. of times daily

1. I read The Scroll Marked X
2. I read the review paragraph above   Rating

                        Total

Thursday   **Date** ....   No. of times daily

1. I read The Scroll Marked X
2. I read the review paragraph above   Rating

                        Total

Friday   **Date** ....   No. of times daily

1. I read The Scroll Marked X
2. I read the review paragraph above   Rating

                        Total

                        Total points for the week

Appointments for the week _____

Monday _____

_____

_____

_____

_____

Tuesday _____

_____

_____

_____

_____

Wednesday _____

_____

_____

_____

_____

Thursday _____

_____

_____

_____

_____

Friday _____

_____

_____

_____

_____

Achievements of the week _____

_____

_____

_____

_____

_____

Reflection For The Week

It is good for us to keep some account of our prayers,
that we may not unsay them in our practice.   —M. Hentry

SUCCESS RECORDER
The Forty-third Week

❖❖

Monday **Date**.............................. No. of times daily

1. I read The Scroll Marked X
   Review Paragraph for the Week
2. I prayed today; I repeated The Salesman's Prayer as part   Rating
   of the scroll but I also spoke a few words of my own, ask-
   ing for guidance in my personal and business problems
   and thanking my Creator for giving me the privilege of
   making something of this day . . . and my life.   Total

(Insert number in each box)

Tuesday **Date**.............................. No. of times daily

1. I read The Scroll Marked X
2. I read the review paragraph above   Rating

Total

Wednesday **Date**.............................. No. of times daily

1. I read The Scroll Marked X
2. I read the review paragraph above   Rating

Total

Thursday **Date**.............................. No. of times daily

1. I read The Scroll Marked X
2. I read the review paragraph above   Rating

Total

Friday **Date**.............................. No. of times daily

1. I read The Scroll Marked X
2. I read the review paragraph above   Rating

Total

Total points for the week

Appointments for the week _____

Monday _____

_____

_____

_____

_____

Tuesday _____

_____

_____

_____

_____

Wednesday _____

_____

_____

_____

_____

Thursday _____

_____

_____

_____

_____

Friday _____

_____

_____

_____

_____

Achievements of the week _____

_____

_____

_____

_____

_____

Reflection For The Week

True prayer never comes weeping home. I am sure that I shall get either what I ask, or what I ought to have asked.
—*Leighton*

SUCCESS RECORDER
The Forty-fourth Week

✦✦

Monday **Date**................................ No. of times daily

1. I read The Scroll Marked X

   Review Paragraph for the Week

2. I prayed today; I repeated The Salesman's Prayer as part
   of the scroll but I also spoke a few words of my own, ask-
   ing for guidance in my personal and business problems
   and thanking my Creator for giving me the privilege of
   making something of this day . . . and my life.

   (Insert number in each box)

   Rating

   Total

Tuesday **Date**................................ No. of times daily

1. I read The Scroll Marked X
2. I read the review paragraph above

   Rating

   Total

Wednesday **Date**................................ No. of times daily

1. I read The Scroll Marked X
2. I read the review paragraph above

   Rating

   Total

Thursday **Date**................................ No. of times daily

1. I read The Scroll Marked X
2. I read the review paragraph above

   Rating

   Total

Friday **Date**................................ No. of times daily

1. I read The Scroll Marked X
2. I read the review paragraph above

   Rating

   Total

Total points for the week

*Appointments for the week*_____

Monday_____

_____

_____

_____

_____

Tuesday_____

_____

_____

_____

_____

Wednesday_____

_____

_____

_____

_____

Thursday_____

_____

_____

_____

_____

Friday_____

_____

_____

_____

_____

*Achievements of the week*_____

_____

_____

_____

_____

_____

Reflection For The Week

Pray to God, at the beginning of all thy works, so
that thou mayest bring them all to a good ending.

—Xenophon

SUCCESS RECORDER
The Forty-fifth Week

❖❖❖

Monday **Date**............................ No. of times daily

1. I read The Scroll Marked X
   Review Paragraph for the Week
2. I prayed today; I repeated The Salesman's Prayer as part   Rating
   of the scroll but I also spoke a few words of my own, ask-
   ing for guidance in my personal and business problems
   and thanking my Creator for giving me the privilege of
   making something of this day . . . and my life.   Total
   (Insert number in each box)

Tuesday **Date**............................ No. of times daily

1. I read The Scroll Marked X
2. I read the review paragraph above   Rating

       Total

Wednesday **Date**............................ No. of times daily

1. I read The Scroll Marked X
2. I read the review paragraph above   Rating

       Total

Thursday **Date**............................ No. of times daily

1. I read The Scroll Marked X
2. I read the review paragraph above   Rating

       Total

Friday **Date**............................ No. of times daily

1. I read The Scroll Marked X
2. I read the review paragraph above   Rating

       Total

Total points for the week

Appointments for the week_____

Monday_____

_____

_____

_____

_____

Tuesday_____

_____

_____

_____

_____

Wednesday_____

_____

_____

_____

_____

Thursday_____

_____

_____

_____

_____

Friday_____

_____

_____

_____

_____

Achievements of the week_____

_____

_____

_____

_____

_____

Reflection For The Week

More things are wrought by prayer than this world
dreams of.   —*Alfred Tennyson*

The End . . . or the Beginning

Commencement days are always fun . . . until the keynote speaker arises to remind you that commencement is "the time of beginning" and so far as duties and responsibilities are concerned you haven't really lived at all, yet, and all the marvelous challenges and opportunities are still before you.

After working so hard and so long, for that diploma, the last thing in the world you want to hear anybody tell you is that the road is going to get rougher, up ahead!

And after working and persisting with your Success Recorder all these weeks the last thing you want to hear from me is that I've got you scheduled for more work, more reading, more self-examination.

But that's exactly what I'm telling you!

Now that you have completed your Success Recorder the first thing I want you to do is dig up that memo you sent yourself before you began this program. On that memo you had indicated what you wanted to be earning in weekly income and what you wanted your title to be when you completed this program.

Like those push-ups, I'll wager you did a lot better than you thought you'd do. *Now, do it again.* Send yourself a similar memo spelling out specifically what you want to be earning in income and what you want your title to be one year from the date of your memo. If you like, also include some other 12-month objectives as material rewards for your courage and hard work . . . a vacation in Acapulco, a new Datsun 240-Z, that mink coat you've been telling "Mama" she was going to get, some day.

But what force will continue to motivate and spur you onward for another year now that you have completed *The Greatest Secret In The World?* What have I got up my sleeve for you, now?

In the next twelve months I want you to read as many as you can of the twelve greatest self-help, self-knowledge, and self-inspirational books ever written. Admittedly, naming any twelve books as the "greatest" in any category is an exercise in impudence on my part and my judgment is purely subjective. However, in nearly a decade of editing self-help material it is reasonably safe to say that nearly every so-called self-help "classic" has crossed my desk. From Franklin's "Autobiography," Great Britain's Samuel Smiles and his "Self-Help," Marden's "Pushing To The Front" down through the Shermans, Bristols, Carnegies, Hills, Peales, and Stones to some of the present and unfortunately different group of "motivators" who write books with exotic titles like, "How To Invigorate The Psychic Power Of Your Liver To Dynamically Master Others" . . . hundreds of books have been read by me and considered for possible excerption in *Success Unlimited Magazine.* What I hope to do for you, with the list I am about to suggest, is to save you many hours of non-profitable reading by helping you avoid the considerable amount of tripe that is being hustled today under the guise of "self-help literature." Just remember that every book which begins with "How to . . ." won't make you a millionaire or a saint.

Although some of this list may be out of print I'm sure you will find many of them at your local library. Regular visits to your library is a habit you should develop, anyway, if you're not already doing it.

Here are my selections, not in any preferential order, for they're all great:

The Twelve Greatest Self-Help Books

The Autobiography of Benjamin Franklin	by Benjamin Franklin
Think And Grow Rich	by Napoleon Hill
Success Through A Positive Mental Attitude	by W. Clement Stone and Napoleon Hill
The Power Of Faith	by Louis Binstock
Your Greatest Power	by J. Martin Kohe
I Dare You	by William Danforth
Acres Of Diamonds	by Russell H. Conwell
The Ability To Love	by Dr. Allan Fromme
How I Raised Myself From Failure To Success In Selling	by Frank Bettger
The Magic Power Of Emotional Appeal	by Roy Garn
As A Man Thinketh	by James E. Allen

But that's only eleven, you say. Well . . . the odds are excellent that you already have the twelfth one in your home. Perhaps you haven't opened it for years but it's there, waiting patiently to serve you . . . and it is the unlimited reservoir which has been used, and will be used, for nearly every self-help book . . . the Holy Bible.

I would also hope, if you haven't already, that somewhere along the way you manage to read the book, *The Greatest Salesman In The World*, for a deeper insight into the ten scrolls with which you have lived for so long.

Before our final parting let me give you a word of warning so that you will be armed to defend yourself against those who put down all self-help literature as the destroyer of moral values and voice of the materialistic "establishment." Every few years some writer, usually an associate professor with a foundation grant, puts together a volume which rips into every self-help author and inspirational book ever written. The private life of Horatio Alger is gleefully exposed, Benjamin Franklin is painted as a snob with a phony "homespun" exterior, Andrew Carnegie with a schizo-type personality, Norman Vincent Peale as a materialistic businessman masquerading as a preacher, Orison Swett Marden as a bumbling editor, and Dale Carnegie as a seducer of man's ego.

These anti-self-help books follow a common course whose logic is as follows: America is not, and never was, a great country except in the materialistic sense and since the self-help writings of the past hundred years have been credited with creating much of the motivation which produced our tremendous materialistic success then the self-help writings must accept a considerable portion of the blame for the "terrible" condition our country is in, today.

To supply you with a biographical sketch of every American whose success story and contributions to mankind are a rebuttal to this warped logic would fill your living room with books.

But what is most interesting to me is that this small group of "anti" writers have been blinded by their own prejudices so that they fail to realize that in order to complete their *own* book they needed to apply nearly all the virtues such as persistence, hard work, faith, courage, industry, resolution, order, sincerity, concentration, and action which they condemn others for suggesting we use.

The "anti" writers, in the final reckoning, are perfect examples that what they say won't work *does work!* Oh, ye of little faith . . .

I must leave you, now, and I can think of no better way than with the words of Dr. Reinhold Niebuhr at another commencement exercise, many years ago:

"Nothing that is worth doing can be accomplished in your lifetime; therefore you will have to be saved by hope. Nothing that is beautiful will make sense in the immediate instance; therefore, you must be saved by faith. Nothing that is worth doing can be done alone, but has to be done with others; therefore you must be saved by love."

Peace!

EXCLUSIVE
THE PERFECT GIFT FOR EVERY SALESMAN
(even if he buys it for himself)

A Rare Parchment Scroll...

THE SALESMAN'S PRAYER

The heart of two bestsellers is now an art treasure! Master scroll maker, Jan Wolkowski, has transformed The Salesman's Prayer, from Og Mandino's bestselling book classics, *The Greatest Salesman In The World* and *The Greatest Secret In The World,* into a unique work of art by painstakingly hand lettering the entire 387 word prayer on a scroll in a style reminiscent of biblical copyists who served in medieval monasteries.

Through an exclusive arrangement with the author and publisher we are proud to offer perfect replicas of this original masterpiece, measuring a huge 14 by 18 inches on the finest durable parchment which we have process aged until each copy has the texture, the richness, even the color of an ancient manuscript resurrected from that time when The Salesman's Prayer was first spoken.

Your beautiful Salesman's Prayer antique parchment scroll will be mailed to you, unfolded and carefully rolled in a sturdy mailing tube, ready for framing, to become the permanent focus of attention in any home or office.

The price...only $3.00 each, postpaid. Suggestion: order more than one, for they make distinctive and long remembered gifts which will continue to provide a lifetime of inspiration and hope to everyone you know who must deal with others in order to earn his or her daily bread. Each scroll of your "more than one" order will be mailed to you separately in its own gift tube.

THE PERFECT GIFT

For the first time Og Mandino's three great hardcover inspirational classics, *The Greatest Salesman in the World, The Greatest Secret in the World,* and *The Greatest Miracle in the World,* have been packaged within the most striking leatherette slipcase ever custom crafted for any book set.

On the face of this specially designed case is an embossed, hand illuminated scroll of "The Salesman's Prayer." On the reverse is Og Mandino's raised signature.

These three masterpieces, over the past seven years, have already sold more than 2,100,000 copies! How many lives they have changed for the better is impossible to calculate.

This is the ultimate gift.

At All Bookstores